Retrievers & Retrieving

By

MAJOR W.G. ELEY

Vintage Dog Books
Home Farm
44 Evesham Road
Cookhill, Alcester
Warwickshire
B49 5LJ

www.vintagedogbooks.com

ISBN No. 978-84664-003-2

Published by Vintage Dog Books 2005
Vintage Dog books is an imprint of Read Books

British Library Cataloguing-in-Publication Data
A catalogue record for this book is available
from the British Library.

Vintage Dog Books
Home Farm
44 Evesham Road
Cookhill, Alcester
Warwickshire
B49 5LJ

RETRIEVERS AND RETRIEVING.

(Revised Edition.)

RETRIEVERS AND RETRIEVING.

(REVISED EDITION.)

WITH A CHAPTER ON RETRIEVER TRIALS.

BY

MAJOR W. G. ELEY.

LONDON :

THE FIELD & QUEEN (HORACE COX) LTD.,

WINDSOR HOUSE, BREAM'S BUILDINGS, E.C.

PRINTED BY THE FIELD & QUEEN (HORACE COX) LTD., WINDSOR HOUSE, BREAM'S BUILDINGS, LONDON, E.C.

PREFACE TO REVISED
EDITION.

IN this Edition I have made some alterations, re-written a few paragraphs, and added Chapter IV. Since the first Edition was published, Field Trials have aroused widespread interest among Retriever men; so much so that a book devoted to the Retriever seems to be incomplete without any reference to this subject. I hope, also, that some of my readers may be induced to take up this form of sport, either actively themselves or by encouraging their keepers to do so.

It can safely be affirmed that in those districts where Field Trials are carried out there is a very marked improvement, both in the quality of the Retrievers and in the capacity to handle them.

When originally written, this little book was most kindly received, and I trust that the Revised Edition will meet with a like fate.

W. G. ELEY.

ESCRICK, 1913.

PREFACE.

IN publishing these Notes, I feel conscious that they are not likely to meet with universal approval. My object, however, has been to interest, if possible, the novice, not to instruct the expert, who is able to break his Retrievers without any assistance from me.

Each recurring season brings fresh recruits to the already large army of shooting men, among whom, I trust, there are some anxious to break and work their own dogs, and to such men these Notes are offered.

To the younger generation of keepers, also, I hope they may prove of practical use.

A vast amount has already been written on the subject of Retrievers, although the breed is a comparatively modern one, so that I have found it almost impossible to avoid a certain amount of repetition, especially when dealing with the established and well-founded main principles of breaking. But what I have written is based on practical experience, and I publish it for what it is worth. It is difficult to avoid a somewhat egotistical and didactic style when writing chiefly in the first person, but I have aimed at the subject-matter rather than at literary merit.

Finally, I offer my best thanks to Captain H. Eley for several valuable suggestions, of which I have made use.

W. G. ELEY.

Escrick, 1905.

CONTENTS

RETRIEVERS AND RETRIEVING.

CHAPTER I.

EARLY TRAINING.

IT is not the object of these notes to enter lengthily into the various kinds of retrieving dogs which were in use previous to the recognition of a breed bearing the title.

It may, however, be of interest to those ignorant of the fact to know that Retrievers as a breed are of no great antiquity.

Before the days of machine-reaped stubble and drilled root fields, game lay well to the guns, and the dogs most in favour were Pointers and Setters, which in some cases not only found the game, but also retrieved it when shot. This use, however, did not always find favour with the sportsmen of those days, as it was supposed to make dogs unsteady; the fact of working out the line of a runner also was apt to spoil their style, by teaching them to carry their heads low. In addition, they were, in many ways, not ideal Retrievers, so gradually other breeds crept in to assist these point dogs.

Dogs that were taught to fetch and carry date back to the earliest days, but their breed history does not relate. As we come down to more modern times, details are more explicit, and, if we search through the sporting books of the last century, we read of various cross-breeds recommended as making good Retrievers. One writer advocates a cross between Setter and Newfoundland, another points out the advantages of "a strong Spaniel and Newfoundland," while the author of the *Modern Shooter*, published in the thirties, makes the very pithy remark that "the shooter may never despair of making a sensible dog into a Retriever."

As far as I can gather, it must have been in the late fifties or early sixties of the last century that shooting men began to use a recognised stamp of animal for retrieving, although, doubtless, a few kennels of Retrievers, pure and simple, existed in the country at an earlier date.

For all practical purposes, Retrievers can be summed up as one breed. We have, it is true, many subdivisions of this breed, but, as each is supposed to perform the same work, and each (according to its various admirers) excels in this work, it is unnecessary to classify them.

The Curly-Coated Retriever, whose first public appearance was at the Birmingham Dog Show in 1850, may rank as the oldest recognised variety, but of late years he has practically been entirely relegated to the Show Ring, and seldom appears at our Shoots or Trials.

Flat-Coated Retrievers and Labradors undoubtedly are the present-day favourites and numerically the strongest, while in addition there are Ilchester, Tweeddale, Russian, and Golden Retrievers. Possibly also others of which I have no knowledge.

However, for the purposes of these notes the one word Retriever will suffice, and in order not to appear prejudiced, I make no comment as to my personal experiences of their various merits or defects. Of their component parts also I think it is wise to be silent, partly owing to the lack of space and partly because I am afraid that an account of their various origins might prove tedious and, in some cases, even bewildering.

It is generally an easy matter to say what ought *not* to be done, but to explain how a thing *should* be done is not so simple ; and in piecing these notes together, I am fully aware of this difficulty. In Retriever breaking, I think that more exceptions to the general rule crop up than in any other subject I know of. There are very few hard and fast rules which can be relied on never to fail, therefore many of the suggestions contained in the following pages

can be read as being somewhat elastic, and not to be
followed blindly and at all cost.

If I were asked at what age I considered it is
most suitable to begin handling a Retriever puppy,
I should vaguely answer that it depends entirely on
the puppy. The disposition or character of the
animal is our only guide.

Bold, strong puppies are naturally more forward
than shy, backward ones; in fact, the former can
begin light lessons at an early age, while it is
far better to let the latter lie fallow for some time. In
fact, it is no use trying to teach a puppy anything
until his brain and temperament appear teachable.

As a general rule, the age at which the instructor
can begin to teach Retrievers their business is from
three to eight months old—a fairly elastic period,
which is liable to alteration.

Had I only one age to select from, I should choose
forward puppy of about six months old—taking
nto consideration the time of the year he was born.

A puppy born after March cannot be reckoned
upon as likely to be of much or any service during
the ensuing shooting season. He has not enough
strength to be really keen, and, unless very carefully
handled, is likely to turn out a failure through over-
anxiety on his handler's part.

No young dog, until fully developed, should do
more than light work; a tired dog means a slack

dog, and slackness should not be encouraged at any age—let alone in puppies.

A Retriever, in my opinion, should be nine or ten months old before he goes out shooting *in earnest*. Of course he can have odd pottering days, if necessary, at almost any age, but much should not be expected from him, unless he is *abnormally* precocious.

The experience gained by a puppy which is just old enough to come out shooting a few times at the end of a season, so as to get an insight of the work, very often makes it a charming dog to break the following year. By that time he should have strength and sense, and a pretty good inkling of what is required of him.

Whatever may be the age of a puppy, a man cannot begin too early to gain its affection and confidence. In addition to this, he should christen his puppies early, and always use their names when feeding and attending to them. In fact, the man who is going eventually to handle the dog cannot be too much with him, either in or out of the kennel.

As regards sex, dogs are sometimes a little more headstrong than bitches, but within certain limits this is a virtue. For obvious reasons, the " one-dog " man will select the sterner sex.

Let the puppy you choose be strong and bold. Nose, intelligence, and the many other desirable qualities we wish for, must be taken pretty much on trust.

Colonel Hutchinson's excellent book on dog breaking is modestly described as "the most expeditious, certain, and easy method" of training dogs for the gun, and the book, doubtless, is full of good information; but I am not aware of any Royal road to breaking dogs. One hard and fast rule, however, is necessary for success; to ignore it is to court disaster. I refer to studying and mastering the disposition of the pupil before any actual training commences. This step is essential, and without it training had better not be begun at all.

The characters and idiosyncrasies of dogs are nearly as varied as are those of the human being. It would serve no purpose to enter lengthily into details about shyness, foolishness, nerves, waywardness, and other stumbling-blocks to success; but I would advise a trainer to be chary about breaking a Retriever who does not show aptitude to learn the work, or who shows signs of some bad fault, such as being hard in the mouth.

Young Retrievers are not very marketable or valuable assets, therefore, *as a rule*, it is inadvisable to risk failure by trying to break a dog which you think will never grow to be a credit to you. Get rid of him as quickly and painlessly as you can. Still, in Retriever breaking, as elsewhere, there are lots of surprises, even among shy, backward puppies.

You are far more likely to do harm than good by attempting to force a shy animal. If, therefore, you decide to keep such a one and await events, you must be prepared to exercise your patience.

The fool of the family sometimes " comes out top " in the end, but I am afraid these cases are the exception.

Some seasons ago I possessed (among some other young Retrievers) a most timid bitch, whose training appeared to be a very hopeless case. Except for the fact that she was the sole progeny of a very favourite old bitch of mine, who was a bad breeder, I should certainly not have kept her.

To make a long story short, she turned out a useful animal, though nothing out of the common, yet certainly worth plucking from the fate which at one time she nearly met, although it took as much trouble to break her as two ordinary animals.

To give another illustration. On two different occasions I practically wasted the whole season in attempting to break animals, though from the first I had strong suspicions that they would never turn out well. Nor did they. Possibly the hope of eventually turning the dross into gold adds an incentive to the work, but more often than not, " *le jeu ne vaut pas la chandelle.*"

By all means instil into puppies, of no matter how tender age, the habit of carrying light articles and seeking for them.   Also teach them to follow you across the fields, or anywhere—provided there is no danger of their being run over.   But think twice before continuing your lessons, until you are sure that the puppy will learn with pleasure and without recourse on your part to correction.

You would not try to cram learning into a baby's brain without expecting to do harm, and a puppy comes under the same category.   We want to have eventually a bold, not a shy, puppy to break.   Anyone who has tried to break a nervous Retriever puppy will know well enough the difference in the work as compared with that entailed in breaking a bold one : one is generally a source of amusement, the other, to put it mildly, certainly is not.   Beware, therefore, and do not store up a rod for yourself and dog.

While on the subject of nerves, I will deal with that well-worn theme, " gun-shyness."

In his interesting book, *Retrievers and How to Break Them*, Sir Henry Smith goes very fully into this subject, and for simpleness or general effectiveness his method of training dogs to the sound of a gun cannot be beaten.

Roughly speaking, the gun must never be fired *near* the puppy, until he has previously heard it at a distance; if this practice is followed, the noise will only sound louder to the puppy as he gets used to it.

I cannot do better than quote Sir Henry's own words: "Take him into a courtyard with a gate to it, or a field behind a wire fence, or into any enclosed space where he can see what is going on outside. Do not restrain him by a cord or chain. Leave him free to run about or retreat should he feel so inclined. Send your keeper a long way off—say 150 yards (the more timid the dog, remember, the greater should be the distance)—make him fire a shot, watch the dog, and you will at once see how much nearer—if at all— the shot should be fired next time. . . . You must judge by the disposition of the dog how much care is necessary: never risk a shot close by at first, however bold the puppy seems; for, remember, once the harm is done it can't be undone, save at a vast expenditure of time and patience."

My young Retrievers are invariably accustomed to the gun by this method, with the exception that I let them hear a gun (at a distance) for the first time when they are running about in their kennel yard; they then feel that they are at home, and do not seem to mind strange noises so much as when they are abroad.

I do not entirely agree with Sir Henry when he says "dogs are made gun-shy by the imbecility of the keeper or breaker to whom they are entrusted for their education." I have seen naturally nervous puppies which, without the influence of imbecility on the part of their trainer, would have been shy of *anything*—let alone the discharge of a gun. With time and patience nine out of ten nervous dogs can be made used to the report of a gun, provided, of course, that they have never previously been scared out of their small wits by any " imbecility."

The shy bitch, for instance, mentioned by me previously, seemed for a long time an incurable case. She never had a gun fired off near her, as she never gave anyone the chance. It was not until she had been out shooting several times—led by an attendant at some distance from the guns—that she overcame her fear of the noise.

I used to have her brought up occasionally to gather a dead bird, and eventually her interest in the work got the better of her nerves.

Before, and in addition to, the actual firing of a gun, puppies should have other minor instruction, and my plan is somewhat as follows. We have all heard and read about training puppies to the report of a gun by firing a pistol off during feeding times; in fact, making the firing act the part of a dinner gong, only of a rather more pleasant sound to my mind than that head-splitting Chinese invention.

Whether this good prehistoric custom still exists in certain kennels I cannot say, as I have had no personal experience of it. Doubtless it is an excellent system, and my sole reasons for not firing pistols are, firstly, because I do not possess any, and, secondly, that I use other noisy weapons, which I think meet the case equally well.

One of these is an old-fashioned watchman's rattle. Such a one as the " Charlies " used to spring on the occasions when they required assistance, or when their generally ineffectual services were called into use. This instrument, when " sprung," at first causes dire consternation among a litter of puppies, and probably tends to accustom their ears to sudden and strange noises.

My other " noise machine " was suggested to me when attending a local political meeting, at which a popular aspirant for parliamentary honours was holding forth on the Fiscal Question, or some similar light and easily digested subject.

The " reserved seats " were well filled, but the benches at the back of the room were rather thinly occupied—chiefly by boys, who kept up the excitement of the meeting by loudly applauding, in various ways whenever opportunity offered. One youth made himself particularly objectionable, in that his appreciation of the evening's proceedings took the form of violently striking the empty seat of the bench with a stout cane, which he constantly and vigorously wielded with a lengthways cut. The result was a series of noises very similar to pistol-shots. This set my thoughts not only on boys, but on the more fascinating subject of Retriever puppies.

Eventually I designed and personally manufactured a machine, which, although not equal in volume of sound to that employed by the youthful political constituent, gives forth a pantomimic (but rather hang-fire) imitation of a pistol-shot. The mechanism consists of a one-inch deal board about three feet long, to which is hinged a stout wooden batten; when artistically used it forms a " clapper," which gives out awe-inspiring sounds, and effectually does away with such dangerous weapons as firearms. A board hung up and beaten with a stout cane would really answer just as well.

Such instruments as these, together with the actual firing of a gun, will generally effect their purpose, although occasionally we may have an extra hard nut to crack or—in other words, an extra soft puppy to train.

The best time, of course, for these violent demonstrations is when the puppies are about to be fed, and the timid ones can be coaxed if their nerves seem too highly strung for their fat bodies.

A visit by the puppy to the village blacksmith's shop, when shoes are being beaten out, will give him an experience of sparks and noise, but care must be taken that he does not get burnt. He should be at liberty, if possible, and will probably amuse himself by eating the parings of horse-hoofs—a delicacy which most dogs seem to like.

Begin as early as you like to encourage puppies to carry suitable articles—a stuffed glove, or anything that is not hard or heavy.

In a litter there is always a master puppy more precocious than the others. This precocity can be utilised. Do not let him have everything his own way, lest you find that he either marches proudly about "with head erect and tail outstretched" carrying the stuffed glove, or lies down guarding it, greeting all comers with guttural murmurs, while his brothers and sisters look on with awe-struck faces. A little interference on your part will enable all to have their share of the game, and the "masterful" puppy, when chasing the others in order to regain his prize, will cause any amount of competition and keenness.

Childhood's fleeting years at length begin to shorten, and eventually we arrive at the conclusion that our future gun-dog is ready to advance further along the road to perfection, and become a useful member of a much-abused race.

In teaching the retrieving part of the business I have used all sorts of articles, according as they seem to suit the various fancies of the pupils. A bundle of a suitable size and shape for carrying in the mouth is the best for general use. Have it made of house flannel and stuffed with tow—or even house flannel rolled up and firmly tied round with string. An enticing smell in the form of a *very* little aniseed put on it is considered by some men a useful addition, especially in hot summer weather. Some people strongly object to the use of artificial scents for training dogs, but I think it is helpful during the first lessons at least.

We do not want to discourage the puppy in any way, rather the reverse. We want him to learn to keep on trying until he has found the object he is looking for without any outside assistance; therefore his task must not be made too tedious or difficult.

Furthermore, after having thrown your bundle, or whatever it is, into some thick, rank, and prickly plantation, you do not want eventually to have to retrieve it yourself because the puppy cannot find it. To have to do so is disconcerting, especially if you are arrayed in thin summer garments, and is derogatory to the honour of your kennel.

I suggest *a very little* aniseed, as it has a very strong smell. This reminds me of a story of a man who journeyed into a far country one summer-time as the would-be purchaser of a "most promising young Retriever" offered for sale.

The animal certainly appeared to have the most marvellous nose, but the intending buyer's nasal organs, fortunately for him, were fairly good, and they *also* winded the object which was being used instead of a " strong runner."

It turned out that this object (I think it was a stuffed rabbit skin) was so saturated with oil of aniseed that the dog could wind the body scent a hundred yards away. When tried on the " clean boot," his efforts were not so satisfactory, and the deal did not take place. I merely mention this true story, but point no moral.

As previously remarked, I have used all sorts of articles when teaching retrieving, the main object being to get the dog *really* keen to find and carry whatever he is sent for. A dog can be drilled to fetch and carry almost anything—including hedge-hogs; but that is not enough. You want him to be really *anxious* to find what he is sent for. An old glove stuffed with tow, or a bundle covered with chamois leather instead of house flannel, is some-times preferred by fastidious animals. A stuffed partridge skin, with the head and legs cut off and the wings neatly tied down with twine, serves the purpose admirably, but will not stand so much rough usage as the others. I object to stuffed rabbit skins for various reasons, but more of this anon. Yet, had I an animal that did not take keenly to hunting and carrying, I should not mind much what I used so long as I interested him, always provided I thought he was worth any interest at all !

Unhappily, some Retrievers will never show *real* anxiety about retrieving these inanimate articles, and if you happen to possess a dog with this failing (for a failing it is) you will find his education a slow process. Still, you need not despair, as I have known animals that were invariably slack about finding bundles, but which turned out good workers when entered to game. Do not let a dog retrieve game, or birds of any sort, if you can avoid it, until he has learnt at least the rudiments of retrieving properly and in good style. However, circumstances alter cases, and you can reverse the above, judging for yourself whether the experiment is going to be successful.

If you have more than one dog, you will find that the green-eyed monster, " Jealousy," often comes to your help, and that a broken retriever will be of great assistance. The dog that hunts and retrieves nicely gets all the patting, praise, and tit-bits, while the other finds out that, apart from looking on, he does not get much share of the fun. I am a great believer in this collective training.

Remember, that whether your dog is keen or not, you must only continue your lessons so long as you see that he is enjoying them. Stop immediately he begins to lose interest. You can either go on with some other work or finish altogether for the day.

The natural tendency of all animals, when they have obtained something which they want, is to refuse to give it up again—and the retriever puppy is no exception.

The first lessons in retrieving-to-hand often result in the puppy getting possession of the article he has been sent for, and either lying down to gnaw it or else bolting home with it. If the latter, well and good. He has found what you wanted him to find, and carried it tenderly (we hope) for some distance. But he has to learn to give it up to you, and that properly.

It will be found a most useful practice to fasten a "check-cord" to the collar of a dog of ordinary courage, not only at the start, but at different periods throughout his education.

This cord should be about six to ten feet long, strong but not heavy, with a spring catch on one end, and the dog should wear it previously to its use in the field, and until he gets quite accustomed to trailing it about.

Shy puppies are such "uncanny" creatures that you may, in some cases, have to refrain from the cord, although in time all dogs get accustomed to it.

C

At this period of his existence a puppy should also be taught more or less to lead on a slip or chain. Otherwise, when you begin to use the check-cord, there will be trouble, and you will find your gay, active " neophyte " reduced temporarily to a most miserable-looking object, with legs firmly stretched out, and nose jammed against the ground—evidently anticipating an immediate visit from Mr. Billington, or whoever happens to be holding the office of public hangman.

In addition to putting a puppy on the slip and leading him about, I find that his education advances more rapidly if you *chain* him up for short periods, especially during his feeding times.

A Retriever, when being led or in the couples, must never be allowed to pull and strain at his collar. You can teach him not to do this by occasional sharp jerks, if necessary, and by tapping him back with your stick. Do not be severe on him at first, as these finishing lessons, in conjunction with walking-to-heel, can be taught at a later period. The " check-cord " has its advocates and detractors, but when breaking a Retriever I would never be without one. The dog need not wear it always, but it is well to have it in case you want it, in the same manner as the groom has the short leather straps that hang from foals' headstalls, to hold if he wishes. Of course, the cord should always be removed if the dog is working in thick cover, or anywhere where he is likely to be hung up.

And now for the first lessons in retrieving-to-hand. Various arguments are advanced as to whether one should begin by throwing the bundle away and sending the puppy for it, or whether the bundle should be placed in the puppy's mouth for him to hold and carry alongside of you. To argue the matter appears to me rather like splitting a hair.

From a general point of view, the method to start with which I would suggest, is to hold him by his collar and to put your foot on the end of the check-cord, then throw the bundle, underhand, a couple of yards away, and, after an interval of five or six seconds, tell him to " Get on." As soon as the puppy has got a secure hold turn round, and with the end of the check-cord in your hand walk very slowly away (or pretend to), and at the same time call him up.

The puppy should not be pulled at all, but, if he wants to " make tracks," in the opposite direction, play him gently with your back more or less to him, and eventually coax him to you. Having got him by your side, tell him to " Hold it "—but in the early stages do not keep him waiting too long. Then take the bundle *gently* from him, by putting your fingers right into his mouth, and keeping them there until he relaxes his grasp.

Make much of him and give the promised reward, which in my case generally consists of a small piece of dried granulated meat, as it travels well in the pocket and is clean to handle. As soon as the puppy learns to return, carrying the bundle, the distances should be increased, and he can then hunt, either trailing the " check-cord," or even without it.

Now for a few *Don'ts*!

Don't face the puppy when he is returning to you. Turn your back to him and walk, or for choice run away, always keeping an eye in the back of your head to watch proceedings. Also make him run alongside of you, carrying his quest.

A Retriever should always return at full gallop, and appear quite pleased when he reaches you.

Don't let him drop what he is carrying, and do not on any account let him lay it at your feet. Teach him to hold gently until you wish to take it from him *gently*. If he drops the bundle, as probably he will sooner or later, being anxious for the reward, put it back in his mouth and say, " Hold it." If this is not sufficient, hold it there for him by putting your hand under his jaw, and at the same time encourage him.

Don't ever snatch or drag anything from a Retriever—no matter of what age. Hardness of mouth is one of the worst crimes he can be guilty of. To my mind this fault arises from three different causes.

Firstly, some puppies are *naturally* hard in the mouth, but with care can often be cured; secondly, others are made hard by bad handling; and, lastly, dogs sometimes are hard on their game either through keenness, or, as is generally the case with old dogs, through a wish to save themselves the trouble of carrying a fluttering bird, which leads them to pinch it.

Once I owned a very good Retriever, who had a naturally tender mouth, but sometimes the first bird retrieved by her in the day used to be badly pinched, especially if she found it immediately. In her keenness she used to jump on it, like a terrier after a rat. She did not do so invariably, but if short of work she was inclined to display the power of her jaws, though never more than once in the day.

The habit which some old dogs have of giving a fluttering bird a " quietus" is probably learnt from retrieving kicking rabbits. Yet I am not sure that when " runners" are brought back dead from a long distance it is always the fault of the dog. I have seen instances of this happen on several occasions, but the death of the bird in such cases is not improbably due either to the original shot or to exhaustion and fright. Anyhow, unless there were visible and outward signs of hardness of mouth the dog should have the benefit of the doubt. My advice as regards hardness of mouth will be short.

Give a puppy inclined to that fault every chance to amend his failing, and by all means cure him, if possible. You must put your fingers right into his mouth and let him learn that he does wrong when he nips too hard, constantly giving to, and taking from him the bundle. Also try pressing his lips firmly against his canine teeth, cautioning him with the word "gently." If these plans fail, as a last resource insert knitting-needles into the bundle, and make him carry it while walking by your side. If he does not make rapid progress, harden your heart at once and have him put away. He will never be any use in the field, and I do not recommend breeding from a hard-mouthed dog. Old dogs with this fault are past redemption, and I offer no advice as to curing them, although they can wear a bit when working, which, I understand, is often a preventive, but never a cure.

Lastly, if your puppy will not exactly carry out your wishes, as you will almost certainly find to be the case, *don't* lose your temper with him. Should you find that capricious article departing elsewhere, my advice is, either to do as Mr. Jorrocks did when he viewed a fox, "count twenty," and see if you feel cooler afterwards, or to stop proceedings altogether until the heat wave has disappeared.

This advice applies strongly at all times when breaking dogs, and is excellent on other occasions, but not always easy to carry out.

With a quick and intelligent pupil the task is easy and progress is rapid; but with the shy or foolish (they do not always go together) it is quite another matter.

Circumstances and common sense alone can teach you how long to leave them to their own devices, or to persevere with these apparently wanting animals.

Whenever possible, let the duffer watch the training of another dog. I am sure that in this manner a good deal can be learnt indirectly.

As the dog progresses in the art of retrieving, so also must the lessons, which should be varied in any way that suggests itself as likely to interest the puppy. Hide the bundle, at first choosing easy places, and later on more difficult ones; encourage him to go through fences and into ditches, also to hunt in thick cover and brambles. If you throw the bundle anywhere, don't let him go for it of *his own accord*, but hold him quietly at first, and then after a short space of time tell him to get it, gradually increasing the intervals. Never put the bundle where he can *see* it, but encourage him to depend entirely on his nose.

You must also begin teaching him to work to the wave of your arm. Hide the bundle, and bring the puppy some little distance up wind of it, and start him to hunt in the *wrong* direction, *i.e.*, either directly away from the spot where the bundle is hidden, or in an oblique line from it.   As soon as he begins to get at fault and puts his head up, whistle to him quietly, turn towards the bundle, and wave your arm in the direction towards which you want him to go. If you stoop slightly at first and keep your hand and arm fairly close to the ground, the puppy is more likely to pay attention to the waving.   Gradually work him with your arm near to where the bundle is and down wind of it, and if necessary quite close to it.   He will very soon understand that you are help-ing him to the right spot, and be only too glad to obey your directions.

I am very averse, especially with puppies, to hiding or placing the bundle up in bushes, trees, or anywhere off the ground.   With some puppies great pains are required to make them put their noses down and " rode " properly.   In young dogs, at any rate, it is not desirable to encourage a high head. Once a puppy finds out that you are in the habit of hiding things above his natural plane of observa-tion, as soon as he is at fault he will begin to stand on his hind legs, against fences, tree-trunks, or what-ever is handy, sniffing towards the heavens and hopping about like a dancing bear.   It is true that shot game at times lodge in queer places, but we need not begin training a young animal to seek for the exceptional.   If he finds *all* the ordinarily fallen "stuff" that he is sent for, we should be quite satisfied.

As soon as the dog fetches and carries well, and also surrenders to you the article in a proper manner, begin to teach him, in conjunction with the other lessons, to sit down when ordered, and not to move until told to do so. Press his quarters down firmly with one hand, until he gets into the proper position, saying firmly, " Sit " or " Drop," and hold up your other hand as a warning. Make him remain in a sitting posture for a few seconds at first, gradually increasing the periods of detention. Reward him for his good behaviour, and do not let him imagine that the sitting drill is a punishment.

Never be in a hurry with these lessons; the tendency of the age is to hurry everything, from motor-cars to Retrievers, and both suffer if driven too fast.

As soon as the dog sits down quietly when ordered, you can begin teaching him to remain sitting still, until called or whistled for, while you walk away ; in other words, you " drop " him. Put the check-cord on the puppy and make him sit down. Then walk backwards, holding up your hand and cautioning him continually. Whenever he moves towards you, return and firmly take him back to the original spot, and start over again. Make the lessons short and easy at first, gradually increasing their length until you can "drop" him for an indefinite time, even when you are out of sight. When you call him up, make him come at a gallop. I myself always run away when I call up a puppy, and I do not think it is a good thing to *make* them sit down again at once—it causes them to be "slow off the mark."

This "dropping" a dog I consider a most valuable adjunct to his education, as it is easier to prevent riot if a dog will either drop, or at least stop, when you hold up your hand and call "Sit." In the case of keepers, it is especially useful, enabling a man to go round inspecting his coops or vermin traps, having made his dog sit quietly until he has left "the dangerous zone." In fact, a Retriever is not properly broken if he will not sit down when ordered to do so, and remain there until allowed to move. You must, of course, use your discretion in the case of puppies, and not "drop" them too frequently, for they naturally dislike it, and they are liable to become shy and more difficult to handle than before. When the lessons are learnt you can go a step further, and "drop" all your dogs, making each come to his name when called.

If we have taught the dog to hunt, find, and retrieve creditably, lead quietly on a slip, sit down when told, and remain still until called up, we have made a good start. In addition, we must not forget that our young friend is probably now well over any little tendency he may have had to retire to the "serre-file" rank when the shooting began.

So far I have written nothing about the teaching of a dog to walk-at-heel, and purposely, for this reason—that I really believe the origin of the frequent cry of " want of dash," " overbroken brute," etc., can often be traced to the practice of starting young puppies in their career with a too strict discipline —apart from any cruelty—such as the practice of " walking-at-heel."

Many Retriever puppies have a natural tendency to walk by one's side, and it is a tendency which I do not myself care to encourage, as a rule, in young dogs, unless they are very wild and headstrong, and even then caution must be exercised in curbing their wildness. To many people this may seem rank heresy, but I will try to explain what I mean.

In the first place, when walking-at-heel the animal only gets the same amount of exercise as the man does who is in charge of him. This, as a rule, is not sufficient. Few men, not excepting keepers, can give up enough time to take their dogs a solid ten or twelve miles tramp each day. Therefore my first objection to constantly walking-at-heel is, that it entails lack of exercise. Secondly, a dog practically learns very little when sedately marching at your side. I like to see an inquisitive puppy finding out things for himself when he takes the air—thereby increasing his knowledge, and learning that he has a nose attached to his muzzle.

You are far less likely to have a wild, headstrong dog at the finish if he is given a little extra law during his early days, and I am certain you will improve his intelligence.

Furthermore, the shy puppy, which is in the greatest danger of being overbroken, either naturally trots calmly by your side in an aimless manner, or looks upon the fact of having to do so as a punishment— an air of disgrace hangs around him. Now, you want to check this promptly and get some " go " into him.

Retrievers have to be taught to walk-at-heel and taught thoroughly, but it is an error to suppose that this is one of the first and most important lessons to be learnt. It is a very simple lesson to teach. My usual method is as follows. The check-cord is put on the dog, and I lead him quietly by my left side, not allowing him to pull at it, occasionally repeating the caution—" Heel." When he appears settled, I drop the cord and let him trail it. If he gets too much in front (which I sincerely trust he always will do), I tread on the cord and check him, at the same time using the cautionary word. He may want to "off" it in any direction, but the combination of the cord and the voice will speedily enable him to grasp the situation.

By all means teach your puppy to walk-at-heel at any period of his life, no matter how early, if by doing so you are not checking any tendency on his part to find out things for himself, or not in danger of overbreaking him. But he should only be made to walk-at-heel for short periods. When you are out exercising and wish to call up your dogs, which often happens for a hundred and one reasons, put the slip on the young one if necessary, or couple him to another. I am sure that it is not a good thing to have young puppies *too obedient*—like the good boy in children's books, they die early. Not that I wish to appear an advocate of disobedience in Retrievers; far from it. Before they are taken out shooting, they should be implicitly obedient; there are enough things to attend to when shooting, without the additional trouble of having to teach a dog what he should have learnt at home. Only a very thin line divides the perfectly obedient from the overbroken dog, and on no account should the risk of getting the latter be run. An over-broken dog, that is, one wanting in spirit and dash, is a quite useless brute; the Retriever that is wanting in spirit is invariably wanting in many other ways.

It is a good plan to use only the shortest possible vocabulary when training or working dogs, and not to confuse their brains with more words than are necessary; in fact, they should be cut down to the lowest number possible.

The following will generally be sufficient to use :—

"*Sit*" or "*Drop*."—The order for the dog to sit down and remain quiet, until told to move. It is best always to hold up your hand at the moment when you drop the dog.

"*Hie-lost*."—When the dog is sent to look for something which he has to hunt for.

"*Heel*" and "*Kennel*" explain themselves.

"*Get on*," with a wave of the arm, is useful for various purposes. If I send a dog back for an article which he has seen me leave behind, or if a dog is hunting, and I want him to try a wider cast, this command will suffice. When out exercising, and the dog has been walking-at-heel, you can release him with the words "Get on."

"*No*," as a general warning that a dog is *not* to do something, that you can see he wants to do. For instance, to run in at a fluttering partridge or kicking hare.

"*Gently*" is a household word to use whenever the puppy is carrying or delivering something; it should also be used when giving a reward, and you should be careful that the dog takes the reward quietly and gently from your hand.

"*Over-over*."—when you want the dog over or through a fence, stream, etc. Wave your arm also in the direction in which the fence, etc., lies.

" *Ware Rabbit* " is my general caution for *all* chasing, whether hares, fowls, or guinea-pigs.

" *Steady* " is also. a useful word of warning, when a dog is inclined to be wild and headstrong.

If you possess a dog worth breaking at all, you are bound to have some disobedience, and you must decide for yourself what form the correction will take. Do not be hard on juvenile offences, although at times you will have to assert yourself. Occasionally a sound thrashing is the best remedy, but more often a good rating and shaking are just as beneficial.

When training or working Retrievers I never carry a whip : not because I advocate training by kindness alone, but because if I carry anything I prefer a light stick or strong cane, either of which, I think, are better weapons for castigation. Whip cracking is too noisy out shooting.

Always carry a dog-whistle when with your dogs, but let it be like an infantry officer's sword—chiefly for ornament. I mean, do not use your dog-whistle except when your own human whistle is not strong enough, or when the dog does not pay attention to it. Let the dog-whistle be a loud sounding one, and, for choice, have a different tone from that of the general run of whistles, so that the dog will always recognise it when he hears it. Make this one of the few hard-and-fast rules of Retriever breaking—namely, that when the dog does hear your dog-whistle, he shall *instantly obey it.*

Your dog-whistle should be used sparingly, but when it is blown it must be to the dog what a trumpet is to a squadron of cavalry, an instrument of command, to be obeyed without hesitation.

When a dog does not obey the dog-whistle, catch him as soon as possible, and rate him well, or, in the case of a hardened offender, use stronger measures, blowing the whistle all the time close to his ears.

As to your own human whistle, you should get your dog to look to you for orders when he hears it —not necessarily always to return to you.

If you possess the art of whistling shrilly in different keys through your fingers, it is quite possible to train a Retriever to work his ground by signals at a very great distance from his handler. This art, however, is not given to all, and such methods of handling are rather beyond the powers of most south country men. Those who have been brought up in sheep-raising districts know well to what degrees of perfection a shepherd can train his dog, and it is only by practical demonstration that one can learn these methods. They cannot be imparted through the pages of any book.

All work in the field should be carried out quietly, without raising the voice, hence you have to resort to whistling, which does not disturb game as much as the human voice does.

We will imagine that a Retriever is hunting for a runner, and you want him to try to the right, and nearer the fence. A whistle with the mouth, and the dog looks up ; you can then turn towards the fence, and wave him in that direction.

Another accomplishment to be taught is to go into deep water, and retrieve from it. It is difficult to keep most Retrievers out of water, but, I grieve to say, I have met others which do not take kindly to the element. With this class of dog, it is best to begin by throwing biscuit or some attraction into shallow water (if the dog is really hungry, so much the better), and gradually to induce him to swim of his own accord, by throwing the food in water out of wading depth. I have also had my dogs held on the opposite bank of a river, and have whistled them all across to me, starting with an old stager. It is useless to force an unwilling dog—he must learn to like swimming. Sometimes a whole season may pass without the necessity arising of having to send a dog into the water, but a good Retriever must be a good water dog also, and at times the latter quality is indispensable.

I once knew of an old man who used to shoot duck on some treacherous mud flats, at the mouth of a tidal river on the East Coast. He was always assisted by a Retriever who was a first-rate worker.

D

One evening when stalking some duck, which were floating out on the tide, he espied another gunner also creeping towards the same group of birds. My old man signalled to the other, and they met in solemn conclave behind a fence, and decided to fire together and divide the spoil. The result was six duck left flapping on the water. The Retriever now came in and retrieved all the birds one after the other. When the time for the division arrived, the owner of the dog gave the other man two ducks, keeping four for himself, which, however, did not meet with the "dogless" one's approval, who began to expostulate. His arguments were promptly cut short by the following explanation: "No, no, there's two for you, and two for me, and two for the dawg, and if it hadn't been for the dawg, you wouldn't have got your two." Which was correct.

All young dogs should be taught to jump over an obstacle when ordered, and to go through a fence or stream. This is best taught by first throwing some small dainty (or a bundle) over, say, a flight of hurdles through which he cannot squeeze his body, or the other side of which he cannot reach without jumping. Make him learn what "over-over" means, and he can then be told to jump over and come back again for his reward.

In addition, he must be taught to work well out in the adjoining field to that in which you stand. This can only be done by whistle and arm signals, gradually teaching the dog that the bundle is often hidden not only in a fence, but also right out in the open. In similar manner he should be taught to cross a stream or ditch and work to signals.

Make it a rule when out exercising never to go back for a young dog that thinks he cannot get over or through a fence or gate, if, in your opinion, he could do so by using a little common sense and energy.

Nothing teaches him quicker than having to overcome these difficulties for himself. It is a common occurrence to hear and see a young dog howling piteously, and making frantic efforts to get *under* a gate over which you have climbed, when probably there is a large gap in the fence a couple of yards away. If left behind he will usually find the gap for himself; the next time he is in difficulties he will look about for himself. If you go back and haul him over, you will have to perform the same office at the next obstacle that bars his path. Acting on the same principle, some Masters of hounds will not allow a whipper-in to go back for hounds. Dogs hate to be left behind, and will usually cast up again if they can.

Every Retriever must be taught " manners," and be accustomed to strangers and traffic. Take a young dog occasionally into the neighbouring town, on a market day for choice, and lead him through the streets. The drive or railway journey, combined with all the marvellous sights, will do a great deal towards expanding his brain.

Getting in and out of carts, railway compartments, and motor-cars are all useful accomplishments for a Retriever.

I have known young dogs, that promised well at home, quite cowed on their first day's shooting— entirely owing to the strange faces and unusual bustle around them. Instead of attending to the work ahead of them, they had a suspicious eye fixed on every beater or bag carrier, who doubtless appeared to them to be intent on harm to all Retrievers.

To teach a dog to enter his kennel when told, I always begin by using a check-cord; I first lead him in, telling him at the same time to "kennel." He is rewarded when in the kennel, and the lessons are repeated daily until he walks in naturally of his own accord. A dog's refusal to "kennel" when ordered is a sure sign of bad management. I remember once reading that all puppies when being trained should be kennelled by themselves, or in other words undergo solitary confinement: the idea being that, if quite alone by himself, he spent his leisure time in thinking only of his lessons and not of other secular subjects. There *may* be something

in this, but I prefer keeping two animals together
(as long as they are not both *dogs*), as I think they
feed better one against the other; also an occasional
"rough and tumble" game must be good for their
spirits.

Remember always to remove leather collars from
your dogs when in the kennel, otherwise your saddler's
bill will rapidly increase.

"Manners" in dogs are just as desirable as in
human beings, and all puppies should be taught
gentlemanly behaviour in and out of doors. They
must ignore sheep, poultry, hares, and rabbits, etc.,
and when breaking a Retriever I teach him to look
upon the last two animals in the same light as if
they were poultry. That is, that they must be
treated with silent contempt, and not be looked
upon as game at all.

We naturally want the dog steady and free from
chase, and we wish to keep all the dash and
keenness in him; therefore, I believe in removing
the temptation from him, rather than leading him
into it.

I even go so far as not to make use of the time-
honoured rabbit-skin for retrieving purposes; partly
because I think the use of it may add confusion
to the puppy's ideas of right and wrong, and partly
because it must surely whet his appetite to chase
and retrieve the "live skin" when it suddenly

jumps up out of a tussock of grass right under his nose.

If avoidable, I seldom let my dogs touch fur until after their second season, and I never knew a Retriever broken on these lines, and worth his salt, who would refuse to retrieve fur when told to do so. He is only too anxious, as we know sometimes to our grief!

I have heard this subject of rabbit retrieving discussed *ad nauseam*, and I will not be bold enough to say that the above method is the right one, or that it invariably meets with success, but I prefer to stick to the "ware rabbit" system until I can find a better.   Many Retrievers are made unsteady, purely and simply, owing to their habit of carrying rabbits when young, although I admit that I have seen well-broken dogs who have carried rabbits from their earliest days.   Those, therefore, who are in doubt, can choose for themselves!

Most people will probably agree with me, that to allow a first-season dog to chase a wounded hare, catch, and retrieve it, is, to put it mildly, to tempt Providence.   Yet I presume that Retrievers broken on rabbits would be deemed capable of this, without any harm to themselves?

I have not enough faith in canine intelligence to take these liberties; and as for the dead hares and rabbits, a two-legged retriever can generally gather them.

To follow a cart or bicycle, and avoid traffic in a sensible manner, are also subjects to be taught. Of course the amount of cart or bicycle exercise must be strictly limited to the strength of a dog, and, in any case, the pace should be very slow— about four to five miles an hour is quick enough.

The custom of exercising dogs with horses, although often a good means of getting them fit, is attended by too many risks. Even trained hunters when out exercising cannot be trusted— especially on a cold morning—not to let out at an inquisitive dog who comes smelling round their hocks. And with harness horses or ponies the risk is greater still. Furthermore, if any dog does transgress during the outing, it is impossible to correct him otherwise than by hitting him with a hunting-crop, which is not an advisable measure.

With an intelligent dog, anxious to learn, you can add to his other lessons a few " parlour tricks." It will encourage him to use his memory and teach him how to " mark " if you send him back for some object which you have previously laid down and to which you have drawn his attention ; the galloping to and fro also gives him exercise. But it is well not to give too much of this work, as I am inclined to think that in some cases it gets the dog too much out of hand, and makes him start off like an arrow from a bow when he should begin in a more methodical manner.

You can also place the bundle near him and make
him remain sitting while you walk away, and bring
the bundle with him when called or whistled to.

Bear in mind, however, that these are only
" extras," and avoid that *bête noire* of overbreaking
if you think your pupil is at all in danger of it.

In addition to hiding your bundle in places where
the dog must use his nose to find it, you must teach
him to work out a line and not trust to body scent
alone. Either get someone to trail the bundle at
the end of a string, and then put the dog on the line
to hunt it down, or "drop" him (or tie him up) until
you have yourself laid the drag, well out of his sight,
of course. If it is summer-time, choose the early
mornings or evenings for these lessons, and lay the
drag on good scenting ground—grass for choice. I
certainly think a "suspicion" of aniseed is useful
here.

If you find that the dog is inclined to run the line
of your footsteps instead of the trail, you can tie
the string to a ten-foot stick or fishing-rod, dragging
the bundle parallel to you and not in the wake of
your boots.

An excellent plan, I find, of making a puppy put
his nose to the ground is to run a drag down wind,
finishing off under a wall or some impassable obstacle.
He cannot then get down wind of the bundle by
repeated casts and so catch the body scent, but is

compelled to keep crossing the trail until he grasps the idea of hunting it out for himself. The only objection to this is that you must frequently change the locality, otherwise the puppy learns to know that the bundle always lies under or close to the wall, and when put on the line immediately "offs" it to the wall and hunts down the length of it.

It is not absolutely necessary that a young Retriever, who has mastered most of the rudiments of his education, should have anything killed to him before he goes out shooting for the first time. If he has been a fairly apt pupil, you will find that he very quickly understands what is required of him. You can put into his mouth the first bird or two, telling him to " Hold it," although this is not always necessary. Yet I think it is much better that a dog should do some retrieving proper before he actually takes part in a shoot.

According to my method, as already mentioned, the wild coney must not be our prey ; out of the shooting season, therefore, an endeavour must be made to find some substitute.

When the "breaking" has reached this stage, I have shot, and had retrieved for me, various kinds of birds : pigeons, both wild and tame, peewit, moorhen, and even smaller fry have been slaughtered in the same cause. Doubtless in training the dog to associate the report of a gun with the fall of a bird, helps him to grasp the idea of shooting, yet I do not think he learns a great deal in the way of retrieving other than how to carry feather gently and properly.

Treat the dog on these occasions just the same as you would if actually out for a day's shooting. I always put a check-cord on him, and make him walk-at-heel in the orthodox manner, and I vary, if possible, the day's bag by shooting an odd rabbit or two, which I do not let him touch.

Wherever ground game is plentiful allow your young Retriever to see as much of it as possible.

Walking through clover and putting up the hares are excellent training for his nerves ; you can also introduce variety by occasionally firing a shot, not necessarily at a hare, but merely to add reality to the farce.

I am presuming that the dog is sufficiently accustomed now to ground game, not to chase it when he meets it in the ordinary way; but as, so far, he will have seen little or no shooting, he cannot possibly be really free from chase, unless he is poor-spirited. He should therefore be given occasional opportunities of seeing rabbits bowled over. When corn is being cut the finishing of a field generally affords a rabbit shoot, which is first-rate training in obedience and self-control.

Personally I am not very devoted to these functions, as I have seen at times such "wonderful" shooting that I have returned home with shaken nerves but a thankful heart.

Accompanied by two young Retrievers, I once called on a neighbouring farmer, and asked him when he would be finishing a certain field of barley, that was then being cut, remarking that I should like to bring my dogs and let them see the fun. He evidently mistook my motive, or doubted the steadiness of my dogs, as he wound up by saying, "Aye—coom you by all means, I'm right fond of a bit o' coorsin' myself." And if I remember correctly, I unwillingly gave him a very excellent exhibition of "coorsin'."

Undoubtedly, one of the best ways of finishing off the earlier lessons, before taking a Retriever out shooting, is to let him retrieve a few pinioned pheasants, especially if a gun is fired before the dog is put down to hunt. Penned pheasants can be utilised in this way, before turning them out, after the breeding season. The pinioned bird should, however, be released in some enclosed spot, where he cannot eventually escape, as a running pheasant will often badly defeat Retriever puppies, and one does not want this to happen.

One wing (or better still both) should be braced firmly to the bird's sides with tape. With the exception of a severe frightening, the bird suffers no harm from a tender-mouthed dog, and cruelty is reduced to a minimum. A piece of good scenting ground, such as grass or clover, should be selected for these impromptu hunts.

I have also heard of wild duck being treated in the same way, but have had no experience with this bird : I am also rather inclined to think that the retrieving of duck is likely to confuse a puppy's ideas. The fact of being encouraged to hunt down a wild duck one day, and possibly of being well rated the following day for chasing the tame article, would surely puzzle him! Of course the respective scents of the birds are different, but puppies do not always discriminate between wild and tame scents.

I hope that these somewhat lengthy notes will not strike terror to the heart of any reader who proposes to break a Retriever for the first time, or that he will be chary of undertaking what may appear a formidable task. I cannot but think that anyone fond of dogs would find himself very interested in breaking an intelligent Retriever; the time spent on the task might be used less profitably.

So much depends upon the dog, and also its handler, that it is impossible to state definitely how long these preliminary lessons will have to be continued. Yet the rapidity in some cases with which the training up to this point can be effected, would surprise many people. The worst of the drudgery—if it can be called such—is now finished, confidence and good relations have been established, we hope, between the dog and his handler, and we now need only look forward to completing his education in the shooting-field.

———————

CHAPTER II.

WORK IN THE FIELD.

LET us imagine that the foregoing training has been carried out during the Spring and Summer months, and that the dog now has been sufficiently handled to allow of his taking part in some shooting proper.

In recent years the term " Spring broken " has been applied sometimes to Retrievers who have reached this stage of their education. Surely this is wrong, if not misleading! " Half-broken " is a better term.

Many young Retrievers, on their first day's shooting, acquit themselves extremely well; in fact, they are quite a useful adjunct to the party. But the smaller and quieter the shoot which a young Retriever attends for the first two or three times the quicker will he learn his business, and the better, also, if the man handling the dog does not actually shoot, but gives up his undivided attention to his pupil. With keepers this naturally would be the case, as far as the shooting goes, and as to the " undivided attention " they must fit in their dog-breaking with their other duties, so that neither need perceptibly suffer.

To forego his shooting is not always feasible, nor is it *really* necessary to a shooting man, who likes to break his own dog (and I grieve to say that the number is very limited). Therefore, let him by all means have the young one out on the first opportunity. In the first opportunity I do not, however, include grouse-driving, a most charming form of sport, but which is the very worst possible beginning of a Retriever's education.

He is generally shut up in a butt, and cannot see what is going on, with the result that he either becomes wild with excitement or frightened at the continuous shooting. Even if neither of these contingencies happens, he will learn little or nothing to his advantage after the drive is over. The "pick up" is always hurried through, and, owing to the number of birds down, it is necessary that it should be so. The dog gets far more birds to retrieve than he ought to have, and begins to get very careless, and most probably slack. Dead grouse are difficult to see lying in the heather, and therefore one cannot pick up many birds by hand, as is so often the case when partridge-driving. As a matter of fact, no kind of shooting tries more highly the stamina of any Retriever than, say, two consecutive days' grouse-driving in August on a good moor, especially if the weather is hot.

Another disadvantage is, that where the same butts are used for two consecutive drives, which is often the case, the ground gets very foiled after the first drive.

More than once I have taken a young Retriever grouse-driving in company with an old stager, but always for some specific reason, and not with the idea of teaching the younster much.

There is no reason why a keeper attending a grouse-drive (otherwise than as a loader) should not be accompanied by a young Retriever, provided he does not let the dog do too much work, and takes care that what work he does is done properly.

A keeper has many advantages. He is able to walk or stand on the flanks of the drive, well away from "the firing line," and allow his dog to watch quietly what is happening. He can mark birds fallen far out, and an occasional quiet hunt for these is excellent practice, as the grouse is a capital bird for a Retriever to try his apprentice hand at.

In direct opposition to grouse-driving, walking up grouse and shooting them over dogs, or, as it is sometimes slightingly termed by those who fail to appreciate its pleasures, "dogging a moor," form a good medium for starting a young Retriever on his career. This kind of shooting is invaluable in many ways for Retriever training. Firstly, a young dog can be started a month earlier than is usually the case, which is a great pull in his favour, both with a view to learning his trade and getting into condition. Secondly, if you are shooting over dogs, a keen Retriever will be steadied immensely if you make him sit down a short distance from the "point" while you walk up to it, whistling him to you when you want him.

Scotch moors especially seem to carry a good scent, and grouse, in my opinion, are stronger scenting birds than either partridges or pheasants, and they are not powerful runners like the above. These facts are in favour of a puppy, and a few easy chances at runners early in his career teach him a great deal and put him into good heart. Another advantage is that a grouse is comparatively large and hard feathered, therefore a young dog is less likely to nip the bird, as sometimes happens when a keen dog and a tender partridge meet in a thick field of roots. Not for one moment do I suggest that a Retriever can be thoroughly or properly broken on grouse alone, in fact, it is impossible; but a dog is lucky who has the advantage of the walking up of grouse at the commencement of his career.

Undoubtedly the best training for a young Retriever is the walking up of partridges in September: a form of shooting which teaches dogs quickest to use their noses, and always to depend on them. A Retriever,

E

when hunting in thick cover, very soon gets out of the puppy habit of standing and looking around him for a lost bird.

So much driving takes place nowadays that in some counties it is hardly possible to walk up birds. Yet the Retriever man, whenever the opportunity occurs, should work his young dog by walking up birds, especially if he wants the dog to make a good beginning to be followed by a more or less successful ending.

It stands to reason that a young dog can learn more quickly if he begins by retrieving birds soon after they have fallen, than if they had been lying for a long while on the ground. Compared with retrieving after a drive is over, the scent is stronger, and he has a fair chance of working out the line of a runner. Furthermore, in walking up, the birds are generally shot in roots, or some cover, while the exact opposite happens in driving. Dead birds, lying in the open, never taught anything to either a young or an old dog; while a strong runner, that has got five or ten minutes start, will more often than not defeat the best young (and sometimes old) Retriever that ever wore a collar.

Other arguments could be brought forward, but they are not necessary.

Whatever the form of shooting be on which the dog commences, it will be necessary to take a little extra trouble if we want to bring him up to our ideal of a good Retriever; but, if we are lucky enough to have a really promising young dog to work on, the extra trouble will be very considerably repaid by the interest and amusement afforded us.

I cannot help thinking that many men would continue shooting much later in their lives, if they were keen on dogs. The day comes when all men find that they cannot hold their guns as of yore, and they either gradually " slack off," or retire from shooting entirely, feeling that they have had their innings and not wishing to play minor parts.

I am quite sure that a man keen on watching dogs work gets a pleasure from this hobby in addition to that which he gains from the shooting. The small days are just as enjoyable as the big ones, if the " young un " is doing well. A pretty piece of retrieving by a puppy will often send one home quite pleased with the world in general, no matter what the sport has been.

Unless a man goes out solely for the purpose of dog-breaking, he should not, in my opinion, make the shooting subservient to the breaking, whether he be host or humble guest. Keepers also generally have other duties to attend to, in addition to dog-breaking pure and simple.

Give young dogs all the chances you can, but in doing so do not upset or spoil your friends' sport.

E 2

All men are not " Caniacs," and, however willing they may be that the dog should learn his trade, they have their limits of patience.   It does not conduce to harmony if men are kept waiting for what they consider an unduly long time, but which you, in the ardour of the chase, possibly think " all too short "—especially if, in the end, you have failed to find the bird.

Whenever I am out shooting and working a young dog, or one which I cannot trust to be really steady, I take a check-cord with me ; I also carry across my shoulder a very useful form of slip, invented by a well-known Retriever enthusiast and sold by Mr. Andrews, Saddler, High Street, Colchester, at a very moderate price.   When purchasing a dog slip do not be beguiled into getting one of those articles which savour more of greyhounds than Retrievers—I mean a slip that has to be pulled with a jerk before the dog can be loosed; this article is not only more costly, but the principle of it is utterly wrong.

Should I think that the dog may require chastisement during the day—and one must not shut one's eyes even to these unpleasant eventualities, I carry also a stoutish cane about twenty inches long, hung by a loop to a leather belt round my waist.   Add a dog whistle attached to a strap or watch chain—*et voila tout !*

I invariably take the slip, when working *any* dog. It may prove useful, and is no trouble to carry.

As previously mentioned, walking up partridges is by far the best schooling for a young Retriever. We will imagine, therefore, that the animal, which has been carefully handled during the "off" season, makes his *début* among the turnip and potato drills—a preliminary canter among grouse having been denied to him, owing to reasons over which we have no control.

A first-rate commencement would be two or three short and early mornings in September, the handler himself not shooting, accompanied only by one "gun" and someone to carry game, etc. I say early mornings, as one naturally wishes to get the benefit of as good a "scent" as possible, before it has been dispelled by the sun.

Should you own a keen and excitable dog, of no matter what age, he should always have a certain amount of exercise in the morning, before appearing in the shooting-field. The exercise, of course, must be in proportion to the strength and character of the dog, and to the amount of work which will be expected of him during the day. To take a strong, bouncing young dog straight out of a kennel or cart, and to expect him to settle at once into a sedate and well-behaved animal amid strange dogs and scenes, is not fair. Retrievers, fortunately, are not as a rule quarrelsome by nature, but when "Greek meets Greek," both overflowing with animal spirits, small differences may arise, to be settled only in mortal combat: and this sort of thing should be avoided. Let your dog, therefore, either run alongside of your cart for the last mile, or work off in some way a little of his superfluous steam beforehand.

As soon as a start is made, put the young dog on the slip and make him walk quietly at your left side.

I have often listened to the "no-slip" theory, but I cannot see the advantage in not using a slip to start with—in fact, its absence is a disadvantage. You want your young dog under complete control, and you do not wish to quarrel with him more than is absolutely necessary. The fact that he has been led on a slip to start with will not make him wild, unless you abuse this very useful check to bad behaviour; and a man who would do this is just as likely to spoil his dog without a slip as with one.

If a shooting man attends a friend's shoot, accompanied by a keen young dog (and all young dogs *should* be keen), which suddenly begins to play tricks, it is extremely annoying to be without a slip with which to curb the impetuosity of his charge. A keeper also may probably get into trouble for bringing out "that wild brute," and even a host himself feels rather abashed if he cannot control the vagaries of his own "treasure."

Horse-breakers invariably take extra precautions, when putting a "young un" into harness for the first few times. Why, therefore, should one not do the same with Retrievers—even if only for the comfort of oneself and friends ?

But to return to the young Retriever just embarking on his career proper, and we will presume now attending a *bonâ fide* day's shooting as apart from any home training that he has previously had. Do not be in a hurry about the retrieving—let the dog watch the shooting at first, and only when he seems nicely settled and to have grasped what is going on, let him pick up a bird or two. Should he have never lifted any game before, commence by leading him up to where a *dead* bird has fallen, and either put it in his mouth—making him carry it by your side—or, let him pick it up for himself. But whichever course you adopt, the dog must hold the bird gently, until it is taken from him. As soon as he does this properly, and also will walk quietly at heel, you can advance another step, by taking the slip off him and substituting the check-cord. You may possibly find that a check-cord will hang him up at times in thick crops like potatoes, but you must use your judgment as to when it is necessary to take it off. A word about taking off and putting on the slip or checkcord — *whenever* you unfasten the hook from the dog's collar, you should do it very quietly, and never when the animal is straining at the cord. Remember that a Retriever should never be allowed to strain at a cord or chain. In fact, you should release the dog—if possible—without his knowing it. Talk to him and pat him on the shoulder, pressing the spring of the hook at the same time. As soon as he is loose, on no account let him quit your side, but always make him walk-to-heel, for a few paces at any rate, before allowing him to hunt. Otherwise you will be brewing trouble, as to slip a Retriever like a greyhound is not only an abuse of the usefulness of the slip, but it tends to teach the dog to run in, whenever it is subsequently taken off him.

Always, to begin with, make him walk-at-heel close up to where the bird fell *dead*, and then let him hunt round you, taking care to walk away from him as soon as he gets hold of the bird, so that he will return to you as fast as ever he can.

I have laid stress on the word *dead*, because, to start with, you want him to hunt closely and diligently—not to make wild casts and gradually get out of hand, and find himself in the middle of a fresh covey, or with a big brown hare jumping up under his nose.

These little accidents are bound to happen, but it is advisable not to run more risks at first than are necessary. One cannot be always sure that a bird is dead, and therefore do not let the dog hunt at this stage for birds that look like possible runners. It is extremely doubtful if your young Retriever will

retrieve a strong runner on his first day's shooting;
even if he does, it will be more through luck than
natural aptitude. Some puppies do not care about
picking up a live bird for the first time; but they very
soon cure themselves of this little failing.

Young dogs often are slow at marking the fall of a
bird, and they require some outside help, in the shape
of taking them close to the fall before they are allowed
to hunt. You must not work on hard-and-fast lines—
nor even listen to all that is written in books—but
must carefully watch the dog's behaviour, and, the
moment you think he can be trusted a step further,
send him in—a short distance at first—to the fall of
the bird. Otherwise, if you persist in only letting him
hunt closely round you, it is probable that he will
eventually degenerate into a regular potterer, and will
spend his time sniffing round and round one
particular turnip root, as if the bird had gone to
ground and required digging.

It may be some days before you can trust him to
go in, say, fifteen or twenty yards, to the fall; or he
may show such natural quickness and intelligence
on his first day's shooting, that you feel entitled to
give him more rein. In this you must act according
to your own judgment.

The more courage and keenness the dog has, the
longer will it be before he can be trusted far from
you. The natural tendency of young dogs is to

overshoot the mark by some yards ; they may then commence to work away from you, being lured on by fresh birds.   But it is these courageous and keen dogs that make good Retrievers in the end, so, in your anxiety to get steadiness, do not overstep the mark and lose dash.

Never let your dog leave your side, *under any pretence whatever,* until he is told to do so. if he does run in, whistle him back, and put him on the slip as a punishment.   Should he repeat the offence, you must take stronger measures.

The slip and check-cord should be constantly taken off and put on, as occasion permits.   In fact, the animal should live in a sphere of wonderment, not knowing whether he is a prisoner wholly, or partly, or entirely free. He will naturally be taken up with watching the shooting, and have no mind to think about slips, etc.   When he is behaving well, for instance, take the slip off, and let him wear the check-cord.   This in its turn can be removed as circumstances prompt, and the dog can then be allowed to walk quite freely by your side, or hunt for birds.   Again, suppose a bird is killed at the end of the last beat of a field, a good opportunity then arises to let him retrieve it with no cord on.   If you thus use a little judgment when letting him hunt, he will not be likely to get into mischief, and at the same time you will avoid upsetting the day's shooting.

If you find (as it is to be hoped you will) that your pupil is getting a little too keen when he sees birds falling, make him sit down, and caution him not to move while some other dog is retrieving them. If this is not sufficient, you must put him on the slip again. It is a good plan to make a keen dog walk a short way by your side towards the fall of the bird, and then make him sit for a few seconds before casting him off to hunt. This often steadies his nerves, especially if you speak to him quietly and slowly when you give him the command "Hie-lost," and also caution him with a warning word of "Steady." I have previously stated that you must not be in a hurry about the retrieving part of his education, therefore it must not be supposed that all the work above alluded to need be crammed into the dog's first day's shooting. He must only be allowed to retrieve occasionally, the birds being selected by you which you think him capable of finding. On no account must he be allowed to retrieve every bird that falls in front of him. If you overdo the work, you run a great risk of making a keen dog unsteady, and a slack one slacker.

Naturally a man praises his dog after a successful find. A pat on his back and a word or two of encouragement are his due, although the mere fact of having found the bird is of itself generally quite encouragement enough. Yet you want the dog to know that *you* also are pleased.

To quote Sir Henry Smith again: "Every hunt, successful or unsuccessful, should have a definite termination"; and I cordially agree with him. Whenever your Retriever (of any age) has worked his ground well, but with no result, and is called in again, pat him, and let him know that you are satisfied that he has done his best. Try to avoid disappointing young dogs as much as possible: that is to say, if you can manage it, let *all* their hunts, at the beginning of their career, have a successful ending.

This can only be done partially by choosing at first what look like easy birds to retrieve, and not allowing the young dog to try his hand at a "stickler"—to wit, a strong runner or a bird fallen in some thick, bad-scenting cover.

You can also partly remedy disappointment by carrying a freshly killed partridge in your pocket and putting it down previously to whistling your dog in. You can then work him up close to where it lies, and the dog can find the bird and triumphantly bring it to you.

Never let a young Retriever hunt in company with another dog or dogs at the same time and in the same spot. This is a good rule to observe with Retrievers of any age, but more especially with young

ones. A puppy generally hunts jealously when
in company, watching the other dog, and going to
him continually instead of trying to puzzle out
things for himself. Where two dogs are working,
both suffer in their work by foiling the ground and
getting into each other's way, while the older animal
generally. gets the prize, which is not a desirable
result.

When shooting at an ordinary day's walking-up
of partridges, it is, of course, out of the question to
work a dog indefinitely whilst the remaining guns
stand idly watching, and become, most probably,
intensely bored. A certain number of hunts are
bound to be unsuccessful ; so, in order to avoid continually disappointing a young Retriever, I always
make use of a dead bird if I think he requires to be
given a little " heart " occasionally.

Dead birds in the pocket are, I fear, put to an
illegitimate use at times. I recall to mind two
Retrievers who, if they always honestly found the
game they were reputed to have discovered, were
undoubtedly the best workers that I have hitherto
come across. Both were handled by keepers, and
both never failed to find what they were sent for.
A partridge struck and carrying on several fields—
only to be vaguely marked down—was invariably
brought to bag by "Nell" when her handler was
sent in quest. I can see him now returning with a

bird in his hand, and informing us that "Ma batch got un." The other prodigy also used to be taken into the dim distance after such trifles as strong running cock pheasants, which had had ten minutes' law, and his owner (for he belonged to the man who worked him) never failed to bring back a bird. At that time I used warmly to praise these achievements, but from what I gathered subsequently I have a shrewd suspicion that a certain proportion of this retrieved game not only came back with the dog but also travelled out in company with him. I write "a certain proportion" because I know that both were good Retrievers; that they *never* failed I do not believe.

Most keepers have many advantages over shooting men in their opportunities to break Retrievers successfully—which advantages they do not always make the most of. A keeper rarely takes part in the shooting, and therefore can devote more time to watching his dog's behaviour. Furthermore, he can drop behind and work his young dog quietly by himself for some bird which has not been gathered or which has fallen wide of the guns. If unable to find it, he can humbug his pupil with a dead bird from his pocket, but often, owing to the fact of having been left alone, and of not having to hurry the dog within reasonable limits, the hunt terminates with a find.

So far I have succeeded in avoiding the subject of unpromising Retrievers, although there is no doubt that a goodly proportion of animals which take the field every autumn are far from likely ever to distinguish themselves in after-life. We know that the Egyptians of old were unable to make bricks without straw, and no man (however capable) can make a good Retriever unless the dog has the natural qualities in him. A dog with certain faults can often be improved, but how, for instance, is any man going to give a dog with a bad nose (not a bad name) a good one? Shyness at times may prove a big stumbling-block, but if the dog has hidden under his timid nature the natural good qualities, all will possibly come right in the end.

A man must be very quiet and patient with these shy Retrievers, and give them a good deal of extra law: that is to say, must not be hard on the dog for faults committed, but let him range wider and more freely than would be permitted to an animal of ordinary courage. Once you have got him to take a delight in shooting, the shyness will vanish as quickly as the morning mist. Your one object must be to get him keen—never minding if he is a bit out of hand at first. You can "tak' it 'oot o' him" later. Shyness is not want of brain. The brainless dog is a much more difficult subject, and never worth the trouble of breaking. A friend of mine used always to say,

" I would far sooner have dealings with a knave than
a fool. You can pit your cunning against that of
the former, but you never know what a fool will do ! "
So it is with Retrievers. The object of these notes,
however, is to deal with Retrievers of ordinary sense
and abilities, so we will return to the " promising
puppy."

With any luck a Retriever, after two or three
days' shooting, makes giant strides in his work,
and as he progresses you will take more
liberties with him, and set him more difficult
work to do.

The dog now should be getting quite " old-
fashioned " (as a keeper once explained to me), that
is to say, he should be very fairly steady and quite
obedient, and able to find all simple dead birds with
more or less certainty. The slip, at this stage of his
career, need only be used very occasionally, and
the check-cord can be dispensed with periodically—
although I think that it should be used more or less
all through the dog's first season. There should be
no necessity now to walk close to the fall, but the
dog can be sent in some little distance from where the
bird lies. Nevertheless, it is a good plan to advance
with him a short way—say, four or five yards—as
when he comes towards you, with the object of his
search, you can then turn round and walk back. He
can also distinguish your signals better than if you

were standing in line with the other guns, bag carriers, etc.

Be careful at all costs not to overdo the work. This refers especially to dogs that are breaking well and learning their duties quickly, as the general tactics employed are, "the better the puppy is working, the more work he is given to do." If he gets more retrieving than he ought to have he will generally show it in one or two ways, namely, either by wildness or tameness; but more often by the latter. Keep an eagle eye, therefore, on his general behaviour, and note the result of your system of training, and act accordingly.

A whole day's shooting is too much for most young dogs, and they undoubtedly gain more benefit from half-days. During the earlier part of the shooting season, whether you have one or more Retrievers, you should only let a first-season dog do half a day's work—if you can possibly arrange it so. Work him all the morning for choice, then leave him behind, securely *chained* up at some spot whence you can conveniently fetch him at the end of the day, or make some such arrangements.

If, in spite of all precautions, a young Retriever becomes slack and listless, stop his work *at once.* You can do no good by persevering with him, and you may certainly do harm. If the dog has degenerated from being keen into becoming slack,

F

there is a screw loose somewhere. Either you have overworked him, and it is a case of *jam satis*, or very possibly he is sickening for distemper. This detestable malady has especial charms for young dogs of the age at which one generally commences to work them.

A naturally slack dog, which gives in on the slightest pretext, is, to my mind, one of the very worst kind of Retrievers that a man can own. The knowledge that birds are down, and that your Retriever declines to make efforts to find them, is galling in the extreme. You are so utterly helpless in the matter that to *force* him to work is out of the question. You ought, therefore, not to allow a first-season dog even to guess what the feeling of slackness and boredom is like. Keepers, above all people, require high-couraged and persevering Retrievers. It is often the case that the keeper's dog, which has been working hard all the previous day, will be required to come and help in the " pick up " on the following day, and a " pick up " means a series of long hunts for cold birds, without the excitement of shooting thrown in. If the dog is a "non-tryer" by nature, there is, of course, an end of the matter, and the sooner he is despatched to other hunting grounds so much the better for the breed in general. But if the slackness arises in a naturally keen dog from other causes, you must take immediate steps to nip it in the bud. The only way in which you can do this is to stop the dog's work.

If the slackness is due to an approaching attack of distemper, it will be wise to take timely precautions, or you may lose the dog—be he good or bad. A *live* dog thrown back in his training is better than a *dead* one. And by grasping at too much you may end in getting nothing, like the Irishman who dreamed that when he visited the Pope he was offered a drink, with the question did he prefer " Hot with or cold without?" Patrick chose the former, and when subsequently relating his dream said, "Just as His Holiness had gone out to fetch the wather I woke up. And if I'd only chosen cold without' I'd have had my drink."

It is not always entirely the dog's fault that he declines his work in the middle of the day. In hot and dry autumn weather water is often very scarce, and dogs suffer greatly from thirst. On estates where such a scarcity exists it should be a rule to take out water for the dogs, just as luncheon is taken for the shooting-party. A stone jar and a tin pan carried in the game-cart will work wonders. Apart from humane reasons, water given to your dogs on a hot day will have a very beneficial result on the day's bag, as many birds will be retrieved which would otherwise never be found. Furthermore, many dogs undoubtedly are far too soft and out of condition at the beginning of the shooting season. How many shooting men ever take the trouble to find out whether their Retrievers have really been made fit for the work they are expected to do? A pack of foxhounds would make a sorry show on hot cubbing mornings were it not for the long, steady exercise that they have previously been put to. And why not treat Retrievers in a similar way, though to a lesser degree?

We have among us, undoubtedly, Retrievers which no amount of conditioning would make keen and fit, but there must be others which would last out a long day's work far better if they were in the proper condition.

When a Retriever is hunting, the work should, as far as possible, be carried out under the same *régime* as that which exists in His Majesty's prisons— namely, on the silent system. The voice should be used as little as possible; an occasional quiet word of encouragement is sufficient. A low whistle with the mouth and a wave of the arm ought to be all that a well-broken Retriever requires for guidance. Nothing sounds worse than that continual " Hi— lost, good dawg," which I have heard some men keep up in a sing-song drawl the whole time that the dog is working, and which does not help the animal one atom.

In high cover, where the dog cannot see you, or if he is on the opposite side of a thick fence—especially on a windy day—the voice can certainly be used a little. It encourages the dog and gives him confidence to go on hunting without fear of being left behind. Do not move about more than is absolutely necessary when your dog is hunting, but stand still and watch him carefully. In this way you will soon get an idea of his "style" of hunting; most useful knowledge, as it is a great help at times to be able to read, as it were, your Retriever's actions.

The mention of thick fences reminds me that it is of the *greatest importance* to teach and encourage a Retriever to work these formidable jungles fearlessly and conscientiously. Some of the fences and deep ditches to be found in the Eastern counties and in other parts are no child's play, especially when the leaf is on. Retrievers coming out of stone-wall countries, or from Scotland where wire fences abound, are often very much handicapped when suddenly confronted with a fence and ditch that would hide an ox. A running partridge generally makes for the nearest fence or ditch, and a dog unused to, or with a dislike for, brambles, will make a poor attempt to get him out of it.

Young Retrievers, when once they have begun to work out the line of an easy runner, or, at any rate, of a bird that is moving about in cover, can be reckoned to have made a good start in their profession. You must endeavour to make a Retriever quarter his ground thoroughly. Do not allow him, for instance, to keep on working up and down successive drills in a root field, but make him swing and cast for himself. As he gets more experience he should do this instinctively, especially if there is a little breeze at the time : but at first he may be inclined continually to come back on his own ground. To remedy this, you must make use of your arm, and guide the dog from side to side across your front, so as to make him cover ground.

It is vexing to have to call a young dog off the line of a runner when there is reason to think that he may eventually get the bird, as runners are the making of all Retrievers. But there are times when, after the dog has had a fair trial, courtesy, if nothing else, compels one to call him in, and although it is disappointing to have to do this, no real harm is done, and we hope for better luck at our next venture.

A first-season dog will seldom retrieve runners except when conditions are in his favour. If the right sort of dog, he will capture some of the easier ones, but there is no reason to be perturbed in your mind if he fails on many occasions. How many aged Retrievers can you recall who have never failed to get a runner ? And how many who seldom failed ? Not a great number, I am afraid. When walking up partridges, an experienced Retriever undoubtedly ought to account for a good number of the strong running birds after which he is sent, but this cannot be expected with a first-season dog. If during his first month's training he retrieves an odd one or two, you should be more than satisfied. I do not include among "strong runners" those birds that move about a bit, and then squat somewhere close to where they fell. This latter kind your young dog may be more successful with, if he has learnt to use his nose and brain.

When working a Retriever, you can at times help him, but whenever you try to come to his assistance, be very quiet about it, and avoid exciting the dog. When he appears at fault you can use your knowledge of "venerie," and quietly work him to where you *think* the line is.

It is quite probable that you will find the dog in the right and yourself in the wrong—one point in favour of the dog at which you ought to be pleased. Should you yourself see the bird and know for certain that the dog is at fault, then quietly put him right. Do not shout or run about, but whistle him off, and take him quietly to where the bird was last seen. Young dogs should be prevented from getting their heads up, as they invariably do at first, when close up to a lively partridge which they can smell and hear. Experience alone will teach a puppy to keep his nose down when a bird is jumping about close to him. A puppy nearly always begins to jump when the bird does, and stands bewildered when it disappears.

To refer again to the subject of retrieving hares and rabbits, I would only repeat that, if avoidable, I never let young Retrievers pick them up. If by chance a dog does bring back fur, I take it from him with a warning "No," "Ware rabbit," and tell him to leave it. Even this method will not always prove efficacious in preventing a dog from occasionally chasing.

A Retriever that runs in constantly when ground game is shot is voted a nuisance, but a dog that chases unwounded hares and rabbits becomes doubly so. The check-cord will usually cure the first fault. You can stamp your foot on it when the dog begins to make his dash forward, and pull him back, accompanying the action with a good rating.

A bad hare chaser is a source of great trouble, and unless his fault is speedily checked it may become incurable. If the dog chases more than once, you can use drastic measures. A severe rating and shaking may be sufficient for an animal that can plead under the First Offenders Act, but after that a thrashing should be given him. Personally I have not been troubled with many Retrievers addicted that way, but in my time I have seen a good many "Waterloo Cup dogs."

Many Retrievers will not chase fur if the temptation arises when they are walking at heel, but seem
unable to control their natural instinct when out by
themselves. A dog, for instance, may be hunting
nicely for a bird, when up jumps a hare under his
nose, and then trouble follows. The only remedies
for this fault are punishment at the time of the
offence, and opportunity for seeing as much ground
game as possible.

I have even kept one or two Belgian hares
and turned them out in my puppy run. I have then
taken an unsteady dog into the enclosure, and made
him watch them running about, giving him his freedom all the time. The ferreting-out of rabbits is
another trial of patience which often has a good
effect. Make the dog sit down about ten or fifteen
yards from you, and kill the rabbits as they bolt past
him. You may possibly have to put a check-cord on
him at first, and peg him down to the ground.

I have also laid a trap for an unruly animal by
locating a hare on her seat ; after dropping the dog I
have walked round, so that the hare sits between me
and him. I have then called the dog, who in galloping towards me has stumbled right on the hare and
put her up.

It is the natural instinct for dogs to chase ground
game, but with Retrievers this instinct must be
counteracted. In the case of old dogs, a permanent

cure, try as you may, is most unlikely. Therefore, do not spend your time in thrashing an old offender, or allow your keepers to do so. It is useless and cruel.

I am inclined to think that some Retrievers of a high-strung temperament can never be cured of this fault, no matter how carefully they have been handled in the beginning. When temptation comes in the way, they seem to lose all control over themselves. One can only judge for oneself whether a dog of this temperament is worth trying to cure: he may possibly be useful for other work. In grouse-driving, for instance, any wild brute does. He can be securely fastened up during the drive, and then let loose to gather your birds and those of your two neighbours. Even then, if there are blue hares on the moor, he may bring himself into unpleasant prominence.

It has been said that to shoot at a Retriever when chasing is a sure cure for this fault, but I doubt if it is so. I have never tried the cure myself, although I have seen it attempted on more than one occasion. It must be a risky proceeding, but if it effects its purpose it is worth the risk. A dog with this habit is of little use, but if cured he might become a valuable member of Retriever society.

I know, however, of one rather sad case of a man who shot at a favourite old dog of his when running a hare. It did not, however, stop him, and, when the dog returned five minutes later, he laid himself down near his master and quietly died. It was found that a pellet had cut an internal artery and the dog had died of hæmorrhage.

It matters little, in my opinion, how a dog hunts, as long as he gets the game quickly. An experienced dog with a good nose will always assist himself whenever possible by marking the fall of a bird, and when given the order to retrieve will go at once to where he thinks it fell. The body scent of the bird will often be sufficiently strong to take him to the exact spot. If the bird is a runner, or if the scent is bad, as it often is on hot afternoons, he will put his head down and begin to hunt.

You must therefore train your young Retriever on these lines, so as to get him into quick, intelligent ways. He must at times carry a high head and not make good every inch of ground with his nose down and it is a sign of promise if a young dog works quickly, rather than somewhat slowly. In the latter case he may grow into a slow potterer, while in the former, as long as his legs are not too quick for his nose, he will develop into an active and sharp worker.

Very few dogs work alike, and the slow and steady plodder will often help to fill the bag far quicker than the stylish, flashy sort. But there is no object

in having a " plodder " if you can get as good re-
results from a dog which works more quickly. If
you find your young Retriever developing flashiness
with poor results, you must check the fault by
making him work closer to you and in a more steady
manner.   If, on the other hand, he potters too much,
it is better to try the reverse plan and give him " lots
of rope."

When I have to hunt for a bird with a slow dog, I
always feel very fussy, and inclined to go to look
for it myself. My thoughts always get ahead of
a slow dog's movements, which makes him appear
slower than ever! Yet nothing is more annoying
than to watch a flashy dog, who gives one the
impression the whole time that he is just on to his
bird, when in reality he is not so.

Still, the dog who finds most game in the end
is the best Retriever; therefore his style of work
is secondary to his actual performances. But good
style should be secured if possible. Brisk movements and a quick return, the bird being carried
well up from the ground, are not only pretty to
watch but correct, and, in these days of driving
and big bags, a slow worker will not gather his birds
in the short time at one's disposal.

Let us now turn to partridge-driving. Grand sport
though it be, it will not compare with walking up
birds as a means of breaking Retrievers.   But

many dogs, for various reasons, never get any shooting other than driving, and although the walking up, in my opinion, is preferable to start with, I have seen many good Retrievers which have practically had no experience of the latter sport. In most places partridge-driving does not begin until October; therefore this late date ought generally to give some useful opportunities for a little previous walking up. A man can go quietly over his ground, especially on the boundaries, accompanied by a keeper, pick up an odd brace or two, and see for himself what stock of birds he has on the place. Every barren pair shot is a good riddance, and these quiet mornings, apart from any dog-breaking, afford excellent opportunities of chatting with the farmers and comparing notes in general with them.

If your young Retriever has had some previous experience before he attends his first day's driving, you will, of course, have got him well started, otherwise you must commence somewhat on lines such as I have tried to explain elsewhere. As in walking up birds, so in driving, I place great faith in the use, all through the dog's first season, of the check-cord. Whether the handler of the young Retriever is himself shooting or whether he is a keeper, the cord can be employed constantly, and with advantage to both man and dog. Should you be taking part in the shoot, fasten the cord to the dog's collar, and when you take your place for the first drive, either stand on the end of it or (should you prefer it) tie it to your cartridge bag which is on the ground.   A dog will not run in far when trailing possibly the best part of a hundred cartridges.   Other alternatives are to fasten the cord to your belt, or to let your loader tie it round his waist.   A short slip is not long enough, and the dog, if he jumps up, may pull at you and spoil your second barrel.   Furthermore, you *want* him to run in occasionally—just the length of the check-cord.   A young Retriever which never runs in to a fluttering bird close beside him is a poor sort of beast.   Unless the dog is a very wild and badly trained animal, you will not be inconvenienced by having the cord fastened to your belt, although doubtless a big, determined dog, when making a wild rush, would be likely to give you a good shock if you were unprepared for it.   As your pupil gets used to his new experiences, and consequently behaves with more *sang-froid*, he will be allowed more liberties; the cord at first may be left merely lying on the ground at your feet; later, it may occasionally be removed altogether.

Always make a Retriever sit in front of, not behind, you—a little to your right for choice, so that your gun barrels do not point at him while you are waiting for birds.   If you keep him sitting behind you, you never know what he is doing, and are not prepared for any tricks on his part, nor can you watch his behaviour—an important part in the training of any animal. In stepping back, also, you may tread on his tail or toes, which will neither improve your friendly relations at the time nor your shooting.

My reasons for using the check-cord always *at first*, and on occasions all through the dog's first season, are manifold; but my chief reason is, that it is so important to have a high-couraged Retriever, and not one in any way overbroken. A young dog, when driving, meets with great temptations, and if you make up your mind to punish him more or less every time that he commits some breach of discipline, you run a fair chance of making him too submissive, or, in other words, you overbreak him.

Let the dog thoroughly understand from the commencement that he is out on business and not for fun. Do not play about with him in any way, and then when you have got him excited begin to quarrel with him because he won't behave himself Of course, a shy animal may require some encouragement, but the ordinary-couraged dog does not.

Let him watch the shooting during the drive, and at first avoid being too hard on him if he jumps up whenever a shot is fired. Speak to him firmly, and make him sit down again. It must be remembered that everything is strange to him and vastly exciting.

As his experience grows so must his manners mend; and you must rate him well later if he fails to refrain from his fidgety habits, as nothing is more annoying than to have a dog by your side which acts the part of a Jack-in-the-box. Your neighbouring guns, also, do not wish to have their attention distracted from the work in hand.

At the end of each drive, let him do a little retrieving, if you think fit; but do not let him loose as soon as the drive is over, in order to career about and pick up any birds that he may happen to come across.

Either make him keep to heel, and walk out to pick up for yourself any birds which may be lying close by in the open, or make him remain sitting where you were previously standing whilst you pick up a few dead birds in his view. This will do far more towards steadying him and inculcating self-control than all the ratings and beatings in the world.

Then let him have a hunt for some bird that is hidden from sight, and if he gets it, you can possibly give him another opportunity. One bird that he really has to hunt for with his nose is worth more than all the birds put together which are lying in the open. In fact, the former teaches him something, while the latter teaches him practically nothing. By making him watch someone else, or some other dog, pick up these exposed birds, you teach him steadiness—an important lesson ; and a brace of birds after each drive is quite enough, as a rule, for a young Retriever. Of course, if the dog has never done *any* retrieving, except with bundles, etc., you must begin at the very beginning, and teach him to lift the bird properly, and hold it gently until you take it from him ; but I am presuming that he has had some previous experience.

When partridge-driving, time is generally an object ; and, of course, you cannot keep the other guns waiting while you break dogs, so get to work as soon as possible after the drive is over. If you are using two guns, and happen by chance to have used them to advantage, your loader, provided he is a reliable man, can sometimes tell you with absolute certainty where a bird or two fell far out. You can then take your dog straight to the spot, leaving the loader to pick up such exposed birds as are closer at hand.

By keeping your eyes open you can also often get chances of putting in some good work without inconveniencing anyone. A badly struck bird, marked into a fence, in the direction towards which you are going for the next drive, may afford you a nice hunt as you walk down the fence. Make your Retriever work his ground properly, and obey your signals and commands. He should not be allowed to range about wildly, wherever fancy takes him. It is taken

G

for granted that you want, not only a good Retriever, but also a well-broken one, which you will not have unless you take the trouble to teach him.

When walking up partridges opportunities to teach a dog retrieving present themselves, but when driving it is necessary to look for them. So never miss good chances.

One piece of advice I should like to offer, which on many occasions I have found useful to follow— Don't be beguiled too often into hunting with a young dog for another man's wounded birds, unless you yourself have seen them fall. The other man's intentions are always good, but I have often found the marking down of the bird to be so inaccurate that the odds against getting it are great. Many men, out of pure good nature, will tell the handler of a young Retriever where they *think* a wounded bird has fallen, knowing that the handler may like to work his dog. But unless the directions are very explicit and simple, avoid the offer if you can, and let some older dog have a try. Very careful marking is required for a running partridge if he is to be retrieved at the end of a drive, especially by a first-season dog, and it is this careful marking which is generally lacking. As I have previously said, in order to avoid, as far as possible, disappointing a young Retriever, you must be extra careful in your choice of work.

A keeper, however, generally cannot avoid looking for birds whose fall he never saw. He must, therefore, take such opportunities as offer themselves, and must, nevertheless, bear in mind that it is necessary to get clear instructions before starting to hunt, and that if he has a dead bird in his pocket he can always terminate a fruitless search without any harm, other than unavoidably tiring the young dog. Another useful maxim I think is—Do not approach close up to a man who is working a young Retriever, no matter how anxious you are to see the dog's performance. A man when working a Retriever likes to stand by himself, and, as you approach, he will probably keep pushing on towards his dog, in order to give his undivided attention to its performances, whereas he should be able to stand well away from the dog.

I am told that huntsmen also object, at times, to being closely followed during a check or cast, and doubtless their aversion has a similar basis.

As soon as your " pick up " is complete, and you have decided that, for the present, the youngster had better rest before attempting more, call him in and make him sit quietly by your side until it is time to move off to the next drive. Do not let him wander about by himself " hedge-poking " while you explain to your next-door neighbour how you missed your first four barrels and the hare which he subsequently

G 2

killed.   Of course, there is no reason why you should
not give these explanations, but when you do, let
your Retriever sit by you and listen also.

When moving from drive to drive, your dog, unless
you are actually working him, should generally be
made to walk-at-heel.   Put him on the slip at first, if
necessary, or let him trail the check-cord.   However,
you can use your own judgment as to how much he
can be left to his own devices, and, should you think
fit, a little hunting by himself down the fences may do
him good.

A head keeper usually has his time well occupied
during the day's shooting, but an under keeper, in
charge of a young Retriever, can often put in some
useful work at the end of each drive.   Unless he has
the marshalling of the drivers, or some other important duty, he can generally spare a few minutes
during which to give his dog some instruction.   Any
of the guns, who have not a dog with them, are only
too thankful for some assistance in collecting their
slain, especially the birds which are hidden from
view, and are exactly what the handler requires.   A
keeper who makes the most of these opportunities
will not only add to the bag but also to his dog's
value, provided that he works the animal in an intelligent manner and does not overdo it.   Many dogs
are spoilt annually by this anxiety to get the " stuff "
at all costs, and keepers are naturally the worst

offenders. They are always keen for a good bag
(I do not blame them), and the future of the young
Retriever, which they may have to depend on for
many shooting seasons to come, is generally put
completely in the background. Yet with the exercise
of a little ordinary care on their part, the bag probably would not be decreased, or the dog's future
jeopardised.

A keeper when breaking a young Retriever should
have an old dog whenever possible to work in conjunction with the youngster. I do not mean that it
is necessary for him *always* to have two dogs, but
if possible he should have an old stager somewhere
in the background, to take the other's place at times,
and prevent him getting more than a puppy's share
of work. If his old dog is really obedient and steady
(which is not always the case, I am afraid), he can work
the two alternately, letting each take a proportionate
share. To handle two Retrievers at the same time,
by which I mean make one remain at heel while the
other hunts, is not always child's play. But when
carried out with the help of a slip for the young dog,
the task is not very formidable.

After a drive or beat is over, it is usually a case
of "Let loose the dogs of war," or, in other words,
every man present with a Retriever lets it hunt at
random round the scene of operations. Young dogs
in training should, however, be treated with more

discrimination, and taught to hunt and retrieve their "stuff" properly. See that the dog brings back game tenderly and quickly, and does not drop it at your feet, or bolt off at a tangent in order to gather another bird lying in view. In fact, keep an eye open to check the hundred and one small faults, which he will commit if left to his own devices.

As soon as you notice that your dog is steadying down, and thoroughly understands that he must not move during a drive, take the check-cord off him occasionally, and let him sit in front of you quite unfettered. Put it on again, however, if he misbehaves, or if you are standing in a "hot corner," which would be liable to upset any keen young dog's behaviour.

It should no longer be necessary to tie the end of the cord to your belt or cartridge-bag; you can either stand on the end of it, or let it lie close to your feet, so that you can check the dog quickly if he attempts a "run in."

When a dog does run in the length of the check-cord, pull him back rather roughly and rate him well. Make him sit down again in his former position, and caution him with the word "Sit!" in a determined tone. You can also greatly assist him to become quite steady by a few timely warnings, when you think temptation may prove too strong for him. When a bird is fluttering on the ground a few yards away, for example, or a runner is making off in view, an occasional quiet " No ! "—" Sit ! " will probably have a soothing effect.

Avoid quarrelling with your Retriever, but never pass over faults ; and if his behaviour really requires it, give him a thrashing, and let him understand once and for all that you will stand no nonsense.

Steadiness in a Retriever is most important at all times, but steadiness should not be put first and retrieving afterwards. With experience and good handling the former will gradually come, but should you insist *too harshly* on perfect manners to commence with, you will eventually end in overbreaking the dog.

In these days of big bags, you cannot have a too keen Retriever, provided he is under proper control. The beautifully broken young Retriever that sits (or more generally sleeps) at his master's feet during the most furious fusillading is generally, when hard work has to be done, the most useless of creatures. The probability is that all dash and zeal for the sport, if he ever had any in him, were drilled out of him by too severe measures.

A good Retriever always enjoys a day's shooting, which shows that his recollections of the sport are pleasing ; but the " sad-eyed slave's " boredom and lethargy may sometimes be traced to recollections other than pleasar⁺

It is a fatal mistake to send a first-season dog
after a runner during a drive, or even to let him
retrieve anything before the drive is finished. I own
that the temptation is great when you see a bird
running hard, which the dog could catch if you sent
him for it, but there is nothing more fatal to steadiness. If you allow him to do it once, you may be
perfectly certain that you will have trouble sooner
or later. For many reasons, no one likes to give
wounded game a chance of escaping, but you cannot
make omelettes without breaking eggs, and you
must run the risk sometimes of giving a bird a
lengthy start, and of not capturing it in the end.
In order, however, not to appear pessimistic, we will
suppose either that one of our neighbouring guns, or
a keeper standing on the flank, comes to our assistance with a reliable Retriever, and that the bird is
bagged before he can go to ground in a rabbit-hole.
Yet to allow a dog of any age to retrieve during
a drive is a somewhat risky experiment, unless he is
really trustworthy. No doubt many people can
recall to mind instances of Retrievers careering
wildly about whilst the shooting was in progress—
the result of their owner having despatched them
on some errand. I heard a story lately which rather
amused me, as I knew the actors concerned. At the
end of a partridge-drive one of the guns was ap-
proached civilly by a keeper, who asked him if he

had anything to pick up, and the irate reply was, "No; two —— dogs came to me alternately and gathered each bird as it fell."

With a really reliable old dog all sorts of liberties can be taken, but not with young ones. Partridge-driving, in my opinion, especially fails as a training ground for Retrievers, from the fact that the dog so seldom gets a fair chance with a runner. What young dog can pick out the line after the bird has been gone, say, ten minutes? He may work on towards a fence, and tumble on to the runner more by luck than judgment, but it is absurd to suppose that a puppy can follow a stale line with any certainty, and it is the line hunting which is so important for his education. A determined running partridge which has a good start is a severe test for a Retriever of any age. The bird is probably half-way into the next parish before the dog is allowed to start, and it is a first-class Retriever who will make *certainties* of birds such as these. I am told that such dogs exist, but, *mirabile dictu*, I have never yet met one!

Inasmuch as *first*-season Retrievers, on the whole, fail somewhat often with runners when the guns are walking up birds, no one need be digusted if they fail more often still when driving is in progress. But if we keep our wits about us, we shall get fair chances every now and then for testing the young one's skill.   A partridge, that has run a bit and then squatted in some cover, will perhaps wait before moving on again, until we approach its hiding-place. The young dog may own this fresh line, and his handler will then (we hope) return in company with the bird and the "most promising puppy ever seen."

Rather than risk knocking the dash out of a Retriever, I would relegate him for life to a check-cord when drives were in operation.   Compared with the worry of having to keep one eye on the dog and the other on the look-out for birds, it is quite a minor discomfort to have him fastened up.   Not that I advise anyone to break Retrievers with this idea in view, as steadiness is far more easily obtained than good retrieving.   Practically every dog advertised for sale is "no slip," therefore steadiness cannot be very difficult to teach!

Every day's shooting ought to bring the dog nearer to perfection, but an ordinary day's pheasant shooting does not generally offer so much scope for dog work.   Nevertheless, pheasant shooting is an excellent training for the animal's nervous system, and no young Retriever should finish his first season without attending "a covert shoot."   One of the chief drawbacks is, that it is always so risky to send a young dog into a covert.   If the undergrowth is thick, you cannot possibly see what he is doing, and the vagaries of young dogs require watching, especially in a pheasant covert. A fox, when coming into a hot corner, causes commotion enough, but a young Retriever seems not only to upset the birds, but also their owner and his friends.

Even at an organised pheasant shoot a young Retriever will get occasional chances for work in the hedgerows, etc., where no harm can befall him, but the pheasant doesn't seem to lend itself to dog-breaking in the same way as a partridge does. The *dead* birds somehow always lie so conspicuously, and a *running* pheasant (supposing that the dog is capable of making any show with it) so often obstinately makes for an unshot covert, that it is not safe to let the dog persevere in such a conjuncture. Small pheasant days on the boundaries, with an occasional partridge-drive thrown in, are quite a different matter. On such occasions one can often put in lots of useful training, as it is not the number of birds that one requires, but merely the few fair opportunities when time is not of such importance.

CHAPTER III.

OBSERVATIONS.

I HAVE written the foregoing chapters with the idea that the Retriever, which has to be broken, is either handled by a shooting man (in the general sense of the word), or by a keeper employed on some shooting estate. The men who put Retrievers first and shooting afterwards are very scarce, and no words of mine would be able to enlighten them on a subject which they already know by heart.

Keepers, I always think, are handicapped, yet blessed with golden opportunities to break dogs. They are handicapped often by having to make their young Retrievers do work which they know involves bad training for the dog, such as sending them after a crippled hare, or tiring the animal to death by some long and fruitless hunt. But they have to do what their masters order, and they must make the best of it.

Any misbehaviour on the part of a keeper's dog also often brings down dire wrath on both dog and handler, the knowledge of which has a tendency to lead the man to overbreak his Retriever. Yet even in the face of such drawbacks (should they occur), a keeper has chances of breaking a dog which do not present themselves to the majority of shooting men—chances which, however, are sometimes neglected.

I do not in the least wish to throw aspersions on keepers as a body, for in a great number of cases they take an interest in, even if they do not attach much importance to, their Retrievers. But assuredly keepers, of all people, should at least look upon dog-breaking as a part of, and not merely as an addition to, their profession. The fact that a keeper is a *good* dog breaker and dog master is a point very much in his favour when applying for a situation. Even if the would-be employer is not at all a "doggy" man, in ninety-nine cases out of a hundred he would prefer his dogs to be well broken and cared for.

The additional quality of being a good man with dogs may just turn the balance in favour of an applicant, who may obtain some coveted situation which might have been given to someone else with otherwise equally good references.

Writing generally, keepers of late years appear to have begun to realise this to a certain extent; their dogs seem to be better cared for and more reasonably treated now than they were some years ago, and I think that Field Trials can be held responsible for this.

One fact is certain. No keeper, however good he be otherwise, appears to advantage when accompanied by a badly broken or unhealthy looking dog.

The aptitude to break dogs—especially Retrievers —is not vouchsafed to everyone. Most of us have from time to time come across men utterly unsuited to the task owing to laziness, or cruelty, or a total inability to grasp the subject.

Those men who possess the first two failings may or may not be good at their other duties, but generally I should say *not*. Of course, it is quite another matter with the man who is a natural " duffer " with a dog ; he is a bad handler, just as some people are bad shots.

Happily, we have also another class of keeper, composed of men who are keen on the work and train their dogs to the best of their ability, and who take a real interest in their animals' performances, appearance, and health.

Such men may of course be " duffers " at " keepering," but I am bound to say that my experience teaches me differently. The keeper who is intelligent as regards his dogs is invariably intelligent about his other work : the two somehow seem to go together. That keepers should put dog-handling first and their other duties afterwards, is not for one moment suggested by me; but most men can mingle the two without loss to either.

Many keepers certainly get no encouragement from their masters. So long as the keeper has the dog with him, and the dog does not commit any flagrant errors during the day, all is well, and the matter ends. A word of praise for a bit of work done by the old Retriever, or an inquiry about the young one's prospects or health, goes a long way to encourage a man. Unfortunately, however, when the owner is not sufficiently interested in the subject of his dogs, this encouragement is omitted. It has been alleged that if a field of hunting men, after a day's sport, were asked individually whether they had been hunting with the dog or bitch pack, the replies of at least half would be incorrect. We all know the anecdote of the youth, who, during a momentary check in a " quick thing," said, " What fun it would be, if it wasn't for these d——d hounds ! " or words to that effect. A similar thought perhaps enters many shooting men's heads with regard to Retrievers, provided they ever get so far as to give them a thought.

But, happily, there is another side to the story. Fortunately for the breed of Retrievers, there are many shooting men who take a more or less active interest in a good working dog, and, since Retriever

Trials sprang into existence, public interest has also been aroused.

Every man has (or should have) his hobby.

> " Some follow science, some cleave to art,
>   And some to scandal and tea."

I am not bigoted enough to think that Retrievers should be the hobby of every man, whether he be a shooting man or not. It is far better for Retrievers that the man who is not a shooting man or keeper should not select them for his especial attention ; if he does fix his choice upon them, it is probable that their sphere in life will be chiefly directed to attending dog shows, or, at the best, becoming amiable companions " untutored to the sound of arms."

Placing the question of hobby on one side, the shooting man, I think, owes it to the Goddess of Sport to take an interest in the dogs that retrieve his game, in the same measure as he is supposed to take an interest in the game itself, apart from the actual shooting of it. And to those men who do so I take off my hat.

In a few cases where a man has the inclination and the opportunity to devote his whole shooting season to breaking dogs, in the hands of an able man the pupil will naturally progress more rapidly than if taken out shooting under ordinary conditions. Such a man would probably shoot by himself or with one friend, and the day's work would be chiefly directed to training purposes, the shooting being only an accessory.

A Retriever, however, fairly shot over in the ordinary manner, from, say, the beginning of September up to the end of the season, should have a pretty good idea of his work by the time it is all over. He is not likely to be very deadly on strong runners—that alone will come with age and experience; but he should be steady, capable of finding all ordinary birds, and be able to put in every now and then a clever retrieve.

Few men can really do justice to more than two young Retrievers in one season. Two young dogs —neither more nor less—are an ideal number for a man who goes out shooting regularly throughout the season. He can break both without either suffering, and should one for any reason fail him he has the other to fall back on. Distemper may claim a victim, or one of the two may prove worthless. Should his aim be to break one dog for his own use, and should both turn out well, he can keep the better of the brace at the end of the season, and part with the other on good terms.

Retrievers (of all ages) vary considerably in their work, sometimes even from day to day. How often have we noticed that the dog which couldn't do wrong on Monday, is constantly failing us on

H

Wednesday? If we remark on the matter, we are immediately told that scent has failed. But is the change of scent always the cause?

If Retrievers alter from day to day, we may also be sure that they change a good deal from season to season, especially between their first and second seasons. To throw cold water on anyone's hopes and ambitions is not my wish, but it is not an assured fact that a promising first-season dog will turn into a first-class Retriever in his second season. In the majority of cases he improves considerably, but exceptions have an awkward way of cropping up now and then. Grievous disappointments may occur. Two personal instances I can recall to mind, one being that of a young bitch, which turned into a regular slack one in her second season, and the other that of a dog which seemed to lose his nose completely when about two years old. The latter had a bad attack of distemper between the intervals of his first and second seasons, it is true, but the fact remains that both turned out failures, although at one time they were very promising. On the other hand, more often than not, a promising young Retriever develops into a good one during his second season.

It is wise, however, not to be led into the supposition that the animal requires no looking after or careful handling during his second season. Retrievers *always* want watching carefully, and especially during their second season. The chief fault against which you have to be on guard is riot, for the animal is stronger during his second season and more at home with things in general, and very possibly may get a little " uppish " at times. He is none the worse for this, however, and I merely throw out a timely warning, as it is a thousand pities that a Retriever nicely broken in his first season, should be allowed subsequently to get out of hand. This warning applies forcibly to dogs bought after having been shot over one season. Their handler is strange to them, and they are naturally inclined to take liberties with him at first, especially if the man has not taken the trouble to gain the dog's affection and respect prior to taking him out shooting. Let it be borne in mind that a Retriever, if capably handled, will generally work better for the man who originally broke him, than a dog who has changed hands after being broken. The former, trained from puppyhood on the same lines and with the same words and signals, naturally has the advantage ; the latter often has to relearn some of his previous lessons, especially when his handler works him in a different way and with strange words.

Any man who buys a broken Retriever, should invariably find out the words of command and signals to which the dog is accustomed. This may

H 2

save a lot of disappointment and heartburning after
the purchase has been completed.

A second-season Retriever should usually be
handled on the strict rather than the lenient side.
By this I mean that too many liberties should not
be taken with him, and that he should not be treated
as if he were an old, seasoned dog. He should, of
course, be able to retrieve any number of birds
throughout the day, and come home with his "flag"
up at the end of it. Personally, I seldom allow
second-season Retrievers to pick up ground game
but on this point possibly I may be rather prejudiced, so the matter can be left to the choice of the
dog's handler.

As soon as a Retriever, after his first season, can
be thoroughly trusted to be steady and obedient,
he can be allowed to quarter ground or work a
fence to the gun. He must be taught to range well
within gunshot, and *must* be made to stand still or
sit down as soon as the game falls. If allowed to
run in to the fall, you will very soon find yourself
saddled with a Retriever who is anything but steady.
It is advisable, therefore, not to be in a hurry with
this training, but to wait until his third season, if
necessary! To allow a Retriever to poke out rabbits
from rough grass is good training—provided you do
not let him retrieve them when killed. Make him
sit down, and then pick them up yourself, or let an

attendant do so. Always give the dog the wind, and do not allow him to range except in the direction in which you are walking.

I will now turn to another and a very controversial topic. We hear a great deal about nose. I have previously mentioned that most Retrievers, when advertised for sale, are described as "no slip"; they are also usually described as possessing extraordinary noses. Is this latter description always accurate? The sense of smell doubtless varies a great deal, but the breed of Retrievers, as compared with other breeds, seems to be fairly well gifted with smelling powers. Some Retrievers have keener noses than others, and some, of course, are almost entirely wanting in sense of smell; but these latter are happily very much in the minority.

After what we have read and heard of during the last few years, this probably sounds a bold statement to make. Some men have openly stated that there is not a Retriever now living which has a good nose, that the qualities of fifty years ago have entirely disappeared, etc. Whether this is a *fact* or not, I cannot undertake to say, as my memory as regards Retrievers will not travel back over so lengthy a period; but I cannot help thinking that the old saying about distance lending enchantment to the view, may possibly have a great deal to do with these sweeping assertions. Fortunately for the human race,

man does not, as a rule, conjure up in his mind the
sorrows of the past; his memory rolls back to those
things which gave him pleasure or which he admired.
In this way he forgets the failures of his Retriever
in the sixties, and only thinks of the many brilliant
deeds he performed. No doubt, he was a good dog
and one that would be hard to beat nowadays. But
surely there must have been occasional failures on his
part?

I fail to see how the Retrievers of bygone days
can be compared correctly with those of present
times. The whole method of shooting has under-
gone such a complete change. In the first place
there are far more Retrievers employed now than in
those days, therefore many more bad dogs appear
in our midst, which do a good deal towards condemn-
ing the whole breed and raising the hue-and-cry
against modern Retrievers. But to confine our attention to the good dogs only. Where a man killed
ten brace of birds walking up in the sixties, a hundred
brace probably would now—when the birds are all
driven—be the bag.

How can the work of a dog in those former days
be compared correctly with the work done under
modern conditions? In bygone days Squire A. would
drop his right and left, and then his well-trained
Retriever would be sent to fetch them. Time was
not so much of an object in those days, and Squire

A. dearly loved to see a dog work ; so the Retriever was given a fair chance to collect his " stuff," whether the birds were runners or not. That he *never* failed I can hardly believe, although I freely admit that many a Retriever of those days was from all accounts very good, and quite worthy to be remembered long after he had crossed the River Styx. But Squire A.'s Retriever was not asked continually to retrieve runners who had got ten or fifteen minutes' start of the dog. He did not have to hustle through his work so as to get on to the next drive, and, lastly, he did not have such a plethora of game killed to him in the day, as often happens now. Nor was the ground so much foiled by fresh game. Hence his failures, in comparison, were fewer.

It requires a good, honest dog, to retrieve birds at the end of a big day's shoot as keenly and well as if he had had only ten or fifteen brace to pick up all day.

Naturally it is to be hoped that the modern Retriever will improve as time goes on. There is certainly room for improvement, but when abusing Retrievers it does not help matters to compare their capabilities with those of dogs that worked under totally different conditions. One consolation, however, is that the most violent abusers of modern Retrievers are often men who either do not own any or have very bad ones.

To champion the present-day Retriever is not my object, but men should take into consideration the facts I have mentioned, when writing or talking about these bygone wonders that *always* found what they were sent for.

Useless Retrievers we shall always have amongst us ; but we need not discuss them any more than the sportsmen of former times discussed the useless dogs of *their* day.

It is often alleged that a dog's nose improves with age. That the actual smelling powers do improve with age I am inclined to doubt, but the dog, aided by the experience of age, learns to *use* his nose. In fact, it is the brain and intelligence of a Retriever that improve, and he learns to puzzle out things which would have baffled him when younger. An old dog gets cunning, and learns to think for himself, as well as merely to *smell* things out. Given a young Retriever whose nose is good, as we now understand the term (I have banished the subject of those wonders of bygone days), it is, I think, far more important that the dog should be really keen and persevering than that his nose should be extra sensitive. The Retriever with an average nose, if backed up by intelligence and experience, will find many birds ; and if he is required to retrieve where bags are large, he must in these days also have pluck and determination.

The late Lord Willoughby de Broke wrote in the *Badminton Magazine* some interesting articles about hunting. No man knew his subject better, and, although the matter refers to Foxhounds, I cannot refrain from quoting some sentences which are also applicable to Retrievers. He writes : " But I hear someone say ' nose.' Well, I suppose there are hounds more tender nosed than others, and if these are found out they should of course be bred from. But I am not quite sure that dash, intelligence, and perseverance do not ensure what is called a good nose. A hound may have ever such a sensitive organ of smell, but he is of no use if he is idle, shy, or slack. Any hound will run hard on a real good scenting day, but give me one who will try for you on a bad scenting day, who will jump a gate when casting himself, and will jump it back again if he does not hit the line off; in short, one who is miserable if he is off the line, and does not go and contentedly lie down and lap in a pond. . . . ."

When reading the above paragraph I cannot help thinking that any tendency " to lie down and lap in a pond " is the worst charge that one can bring against a Retriever or any sporting dog.

Whether the majority of Retrievers in the fifties were well endowed with stamina, no one in the world can say, as there was not enough game in those days to prove the matter one way or the other. Let us therefore drop the subject.

Apropos of the transmission of hereditary instincts from parents to offspring, the general rule is, I take it, that like begets like. There are many exceptions, but, if the general rules of breeding are correct, it is far easier to breed good working dogs from parents with similar qualities than to breed from unbroken animals, whose sporting qualities are unknown. Even if the principle of always breeding from Retrievers who have shown an aptitude for their calling is followed, there is no *certainty* that the progeny will inherit the good qualities of their parents. On the other hand, I have come across good Retrievers bred from parents which were either utterly worthless for work or had never been given the chance of being broken to the gun. In my choice between the two I should not hesitate, as I think the litter bred from workers would be more likely to turn out well than those bred from unbroken parents, with which opinion, I am sure, most shooting men will agree.

However reliable a Retriever is, there must be times when he fails to retrieve his game for no apparent reason, and it is rather interesting, when watching a good dog, to essay for oneself a discovery of the reason of these failures. Some of these problems offer an easy solution, but others are puzzling.

For example, on one occasion, I was assisting to walk up partridges in September. With us we had a very good Retriever, who accounted for a large proportion of the game for which he hunted. While waiting in a corner of a field to allow birds to be driven into a rough, tussocky meadow, a partridge was put over our heads, which was knocked down, apparently dead, into a corner of this rough meadow. The old Retriever was taken at once to the spot, and although he hunted diligently for some time could make nothing of it. We then walked this field in line, and before we had proceeded twenty yards the same dog made a very good retrieve of a runner; he then got another runner (which had been allowed a good start) right over the very piece of ground where he had failed a quarter of an hour before.

That unknown quantity "scent" has puzzled people for many generations, and it is likely to do so for many more. It is a complex subject, and I intend to touch on it very lightly. Speaking generally, I consider that the most favourable weather for a good scent is when the glass is high and the wind N., or N.E., with a slight sting in it, but, unfortunately for Retrievers' reputations, shooting in the early part of the season does not take place under these conditions, but in a more torrid temperature. Of course much depends on the ground itself—

whether it is dry or the reverse, how it is cropped, and a hundred other things. Again, some lands are proverbially bad scenting, although from no apparent cause, while others carry a " screaming " scent. At any rate, whenever a dog fails to retrieve his game, the subject of scent is often mentioned, and I should imagine always will be, until we have a breed of Retrievers that cannot be defeated under any conditions. In the meantime—like the weather—it affords a topic for conversation ; so things might be worse ! I am inclined to doubt if the scent of a dead bird and of a bird which is only slightly wounded differ ; I have been told that it does, although I do not think my informant explained how he knew. A Retriever undoubtedly learns to discriminate between the scents of different kinds of birds, and also between " fur and feather," but whether he can tell the difference between a bird down with a wing " tipped," and a fresh bird, I cannot undertake to say. When there is blood about, there is no doubt that the scent is different. Various species of birds, of course, differ considerably in their respective smells—some being easier to follow than others.

A running pheasant always seems to be twice as difficult to retrieve as a running partridge. This very likely is due to the fact that the pheasant is higher on the leg, and therefore does not brush the leaves and grass with his feathers in the same

manner as a partridge. However this may be, a
Retriever who seldom fails with strong running
pheasants (when they have had a little law given
them) must have an undeniably good nose; especially if the bird chooses to cross some rolled fallow
or mustard seed in his career. Wild duck appear to
leave a strong scent behind them—I have seen dogs
puzzle out a very stale line of a duck for a consider-
able distance, but it must be remembered that these
birds have webbed feet and do not travel fast.
Many Retrievers object to picking up teal, although
they are willing to carry heavy duck. They seem to
have an objection to them, similar to the dislike
which some dogs have for carrying woodcock.

From a moral point of view, at any rate, dog stories
like fishing stories, are often extremely entertaining
and instructive. I notice, however, that they generally begin with " Some years ago, I had a dog,"
etc., etc. The hero of the story invariably lives in
the past, and the " taller" the story the more likely
it is that the events related happened in the boyhood
of the *raconteur*. When listening to any particularly elastic yarn, my thoughts always wander back
to the following anecdote. During the hearing of
a big fishery case, concerning some water on the
Tweed, an old Scotch gillie was sworn as a witness.
Immediately after he had taken the oath he turned
to the examining counsel and said : " I should like to

obsairve, that I consider it vera hard on a God-fearin'
man, to tak' evidence on oath in a feeshin' case." For
various reasons, therefore, I will not commit to paper
any personal experiences of wonderful deeds performed by Retrievers, but I cannot refrain from
telling one story, although I admit that the facts
related did not come under my own observation.

Some years ago a certain owner of a well-broken
Retriever got into one of the carriages on the
South-Eastern Railway, accompanied by his dog.
Just as the train was starting an old gentleman,
carrying a handbag, hurriedly entered the compart-
ment; he was no sooner settled in his seat than he
began to object to the dog's company. It was too late,
however, to call the guard, and a somewhat heated
argument reached a climax when the elderly gentleman suddenly opened the door of the carriage and
violently ejected the dog on to the line. The owner of
the dog, however, immediately resented this action by
hurling the handbag also out of the open doorway.
On arrival at the next station, complaints were
immediately lodged with the officials by both belli-
gerents; but peace was ultimately restored by the
hurried appearance of the dog on the scene, carrying
the bag in his mouth.

As a matter of fact, I do not think that big dogs, like
Retrievers, should be permitted to travel in passenger
compartments, except for very short journeys. They

are usually quite comfortable when in charge of the guard, although it is always advisable for the owner himself to chain the dog up in the van, and to request the guard to see that ordinary care is taken not to injure the animal's feet by throwing luggage down carelessly. On most railways the old-fashioned "dog hole," into which valuable dogs used to be thrust, seems happily to have become obsolete. It was invariably draughty and dark, and was the cause, I should imagine, of much disease, as, apart from these defects, practically no steps were ever taken to clean or disinfect it.

When sending or taking a dog on a journey, either in a hamper or on a chain, it should be a hard-and-fast rule to let the animal have some exercise before commencing the journey. If taken straight from his kennel to the train, he will not have the opportunity to empty himself beforehand. To neglect this is not only at times shortsighted but cruel. Railway companies do not at any time care about carrying dogs, therefore owners should see beforehand that no extra trouble is likely to be caused by their animals.

Before a dog is sent on a journey, the fit of his collar should be carefully looked to, and it should generally be fastened a hole or two tighter, than usual, so that the animal cannot possibly pull his head through it. More than one fatal accident has been brought to my knowledge, through dogs slipping their collars when travelling by rail.

Even when a dog travels by rail in a hamper or box he should have a collar and chain attached to him, the chain being merely fastened to the collar with the other end lying loose. On their arrival at the railway station, dogs are often met and taken straight out of the hamper, to avoid its being carted a long way by road. A strange dog, when quite free, may get loose if there is no collar and chain attached to him, and a strange dog when loose is indeed at times a strange dog! I knew a man in the south of Ireland who once sent a brace of Setters on approval to Scotland. Not having heard anything about them, after a lapse of two or three days he telegraphed to know if they were satisfactory. The reply he received was, "Will return your dogs when I can catch them." In this case, I think, they had got loose on a moor, and not at a railway station.

A dog travels more comfortably, no doubt, in a hamper, and valuable dogs or dogs going any distance, should always travel in this manner. Cases have occurred of animals getting smothered in a hamper or box, owing to luggage being packed too closely round, but fortunately such accidents are scarce. All dog hampers should have conspicuous metal labels fastened to the lids, with the words "Live dog" on them; otherwise dog hampers may be mistaken for household linen baskets, and treated as such.

When despatching a dog on a long railway journey, it is a good plan to insure him previously with the railway company. He need only be insured up to the lowest amount that the company will accept, as the mere fact of his being insured seems to command respect in the eyes of the railway officials, who treat him accordingly. This system also has a great advantage where the dog has to travel over the lines of different railway companies. Each company is always eager to pass on, as quickly as possible, any insured goods or stock, and the journey is thus often shortened by several hours. The insurance premium, which is not high, amounts, I think, to a little over one per cent. on the dog's declared value.

CHAPTER IV.

RETRIEVER TRIALS.

THE first Field Trials for Retrievers—under the auspices of the International Gundog League—were held, near Havant, in the autumn of 1900. It was a two-days' meeting, with I think, roughly a dozen competing dogs, and although—without referring to " data "—I cannot recall all particulars, yet the following incident has remained very vividly in my mind. When returning thanks for the Judges, Mr. W. Arkwright, among some pointed remarks on various " doggy " matters, stated most emphatically that he was sure that Trials for Retrievers had come to stay, and in addition, that he looked forward to the no-distant day when Local Trials would also take place, each district organising its own meetings.

I must say that for two or three years it certainly did not appear that these prognostications would be fulfilled, in fact the reverse, as, owing to the lack of support from those who should have helped the movement and from the hesitancy of the shooting public, who did not grasp the objects intended, the early meetings were poorly supported, and, in addition, keenly and often adversely criticised. I speak feelingly, as I was one of that small band of early pioneers who had the doubtful pleasure of alternately listening to our dogs being abused and our objects derided. However, the silver lining eventually began to appear from behind the dark, nebulous vapours, or to put it into more prosaic language, after two or three years of persistent struggling we began to make headway. All honour due to those who by their material help and generosity refused to let the movement drop!

Naturally, with the march of time, an improvement has taken place in the *general* work done at Trials, but I think that the winners at the early meetings could hold their own with the present-day competitors, as far as game-finding is concerned. Handling has certainly made great strides, and without doubt the dogs' work now is of a more even character than formerly.

I have frequently been asked how Retriever Trials are carried out, and generally shelter myself by answering that "they are conducted on similar lines to a day's shooting, except that more time and latitude is given to the dogs and that no dog must retrieve except by the order of a Judge." This answer usually leads to more enquiries and for the benefit of those who are ignorant of the procedure, I cannot do better than insert here a copy of the Rules for the Trial Meetings of the Retriever Society (International Gundog League) as they stand at present.

RULES FOR THE TRIAL MEETINGS OF THE RETRIEVER SOCIETY.

1.—Before the Trials a number will be drawn by lot for each competing dog, and the dogs will be tried by batches accordingly during the first round. After all the competing dogs have been tried, the Judges will call up at their own discretion any dogs they require further and try them again. Every competitor or other handler of a dog must bring a 12-bore central fire gun and must shoot with blank ammunition supplied by the Committee, and he must shoot as if he were using loaded cartridges, nor will he be allowed to carry in his hand anything besides his gun. The game will be shot by guns appointed by the Committee.

2.—All dogs will be expected to retrieve fur as well as feather, if ordered to do so, but no handler must send his dog after any game until bidden by a Judge to do so. The Judges have power to order any handler to set his dog to retrieve game not shot at by him personally, and, where circumstances permit, all dogs should be tried in water.

3.—The principal points considered by the Judges are sagacity, steadiness, nose, dash, perseverance, obedience, and retrieving. This last should be done quickly, with a tender mouth, and right up to the hand.

4.—The Committee reserve the right of disqualifying at the expiration of fifteen minutes any dog not present to be tried in its turn.

5.—The Judges are empowered to turn out of the Stake the dog of any person who does not obey them or who wilfully interferes with another competitor or his dog, and to withhold a prize when, in their opinion, insufficient merit is shown, and to exclude from competition bitches on heat, or any animals they may consider unfit to compete. The entry fees of all such dogs will be forfeited.

6.—Certificates of Merit will be awarded with a view to the establishment of Workers' Classes at the Dog Shows, and as a guide to purchasers of dogs which, though not in the list of

Prize Winners, give promise in their work of being valuable sporting dogs.

Certificates of Merit will also be awarded to any handler who, in the opinion of the Judges, shall have worked his dog in a thoroughly efficient manner during the Trials.

7.—An objection to a dog may be lodged with the Secretary at any time within seven days of a Meeting, upon the objector depositing with the Secretary the sum of £2, which shall be forfeited if the Committee deem such objection frivolous. All objections must be made in writing.

8.—The Committee have the power, if they think fit, to refuse any entries for the Society's Trials, without assigning any reason for their action.

9.—In the event of the weather being considered by the Committee unsuitable for holding the Trials, it shall be in their power to postpone the Meeting from day to day until the Saturday following the day fixed for the Trials, on which day the Stakes not already decided shall be abandoned, and their entry fees returned.

10.—The Committee reserve to themselves the right to abandon the Meeting at any time, on returning their entry moneys to the competitors, and if, from unforeseen circumstances, they deem it advisable to alter the date of the Meeting, after the closing of the entries, this may be done by sending formal notice to all competitors that they may recover their entry fees by exercising the option of cancelling their entries within four days from the date of such notice. All entries, however, about which no such application is made within those four days will stand good for the Meeting at its altered date.

11.—If an advertised Judge be prevented from filling his engagement for either the whole or part of the Meeting, the Committee shall appoint any other person to judge, or shall make any other arrangements that to them seem desirable.

12.—Upon any case arising not provided for in the above Rules, the Members of the Committee present shall decide, and their decision shall be final.

The above Rules may be taken as an example of all Meetings, although most of the Local Societies word their Rules somewhat differently and insert additions, but carry out the working on the same principles. In practice, it has been found advisable to appoint three Judges, and to try the dogs in batches of six, each Judge watching the work of two dogs at a time. By this means they have good opportunities of seeing the work of all the Retrievers, and also of their handlers, as each Judge, as far as possible, should have charge of every dog in the Stake at some period of the Meeting. Driving game to the guns and walking in line (the latter by far the best means of testing Retrievers) is resorted to. During the earlier days of Retriever Trials, the handlers provided themselves with loaded cartridges in addition to a gun, but this plan was found to have its drawbacks, as the shooting by some handlers was, to put it mildly, somewhat erratic. In addition, the donor of the shooting—and I cannot here omit the hearty thanks of all Retriever men to those who so generously lend their land and game for these Trials —often wishes to invite his friends to take part in the day's work. So the Rule about handlers using blank ammunition was inserted and found to work very satisfactorily.

The Open Meetings generally occupy two days, but most Local Trials are confined to a twelve dog Stake, to be run off in one day.

I have heard the opinion expressed, by men who have had practical experience, that to win a Retriever Trial requires a good dog and sixty per cent. of Luck. I freely admit that the first requirement is necessary, as I do not think that a *bad* Retriever ever has, or ever will, win a properly conducted Trial, and although the winners, in my experience, have naturally varied as regards their capabilities to find game, yet none have failed to fulfil that much abused term "a good Retriever."

As regards the Luck, well, sixty per cent. is a very large proportion, but undoubtedly there is a substratum of truth in it. I think that I am right in saying that the ancient Roman goddess Fortuna—then, as now, a fickle jade whom we all inwardly revere—enters into nearly every competition, from Chariot racing to a pegged-down Fishing Match. There is always the "rub of the green," not only among our sports but also in our more serious competitions, and so it is rather hard to brand Retriever Trials with an undue preponderance of Luck. At the same time, it does crop up very largely at Trials, and competitors must make up their minds beforehand that the *best* dog does not invariably win the Stake, Luck may help another to the coveted position.

In competitions of this sort, Luck very often spells Opportunity, and a dog may not have the chances offered to him to show what he is capable of doing,

while another may get all the " good things " showered
on him, and at the same time be capable of availing
himself of them! It happens sometimes that a dog
may do nothing wrong all day, but at the same time
he has shown no brilliancy, while some other animal
—possibly not as reliable in some ways—has caught
the Judge's eyes on more than one occasion by some
fine piece of " gallery " work which Opportunity gave
him.

My own experience, both as Judge and Competitor
is that, as a rule, there is not much to choose between
the first four placed dogs in a Stake, they are
generally all good Retrievers, and the best one, *on
the day*, usually wins, while possibly the order may
be reversed at some subsequent Meeting owing to
another turn of the Wheel of Fortune, or some more
material cause. Anyhow, I repeat, indifferent
Retrievers will not win Trials, and it seldom or never
happens that the best dog does not come out somewhere near the top, barring accidents !

The above somewhat lengthy digression on the
chances of success sounds rather like a homily written
to soothe the " disappointed exhibitor," but I merely
draw attention to these hazards, as undoubtedly
they do, and always will, exist.

As regards ground for Trials, I think that the *ideal*
ground is a good piece of lowland partridge country,
lots of roots, intersected if possible with some rough

fences and deep ditches, with a river thrown in, so that dogs can be tried at water.

The head of game is not so material as some people imagine, in fact one can have too much game on the ground, especially ground game, but a fair show of partridges and pheasants (many a Retriever has owed his win, or possibly downfall, to an old running cock pheasant) are necessary, but a super-abundance is not required. I have seen several one-day Stakes of twelve dogs brought to a most successful conclusion at a cost of about a hundred head of game. The expedient of trying Retrievers on pinioned partridges has, on one occasion at least, been resorted to. I do not propose here to enter into this subject, as, in conjunction with many others, I do not approve of any artificial means being employed. Trials should be conducted as much like an ordinary day's shooting as possible.

As previously mentioned, in the early days of Retriever Trials it was difficult to find sufficient Competitors, but at the present time I think that the difficulty lies more often in obtaining the services of Judges. So many Meetings are now held, and so many men competent to judge either are handling dogs themselves or interested in their running, that some of the Local Trials are already hard put to it to find annually three competent men willing to fulfil his somewhat thankless task.

If possible, I think that a Judge, previous to acting as such, should himself have handled a Retriever at Trials, or, at any rate, have been a constant spectator. The time in which to try the dogs is limited, and one does not want a man feeling his way and some what in the dark during the short period of a one-day's Meeting.

Practical experience alone can teach him to grasp difficult circumstances, and at times (especially when deciding the issue towards the end of the day) some practical knowledge will stand him in good stead. Handlers should be given every latitude to work their dogs in their own way, and it is a mistake for a Judge to suggest how he wants the dog worked. I say a mistake for more reasons than one, but chiefly owing to the fact that by giving a handler " lots of rope " he cannot complain afterwards that he was interfered with in any way, or that he was not allowed to work his dog in the manner that he was accustomed to.

For instance, it looks prettier, and is certainly a quicker method of retrieving, to send a dog out from the line to the fall of a bird, but if the handler wants to walk up himself to the fall, by all means let him do so. Judges can always draw their own conclusions, and the less instructions that they give to handlers the better.

Each dog's work should be tried under two Judges at least, and, if possible, under all three Judges, but the latter is not always necessary.

When it is palpable that a dog will have to rank as an unsuccessful candidate, it is not worth while wasting valuable time by having him tried again by the remaining Judge. In short, never keep a bad dog in the Stake longer than you can help. This weeding-out process is generally fairly simple, but the trouble comes in placing the four best animals, and, prior to coming to a final decision, it is advisable for each Judge to write down the dogs' names in the order that he himself thinks they should be placed. They can then compare these lists among themselves, referring to their Judging Books for all details.

The Judges having been secured, the Schedule of the Meeting printed and circulated, it now only remains for would-be competitors to apply for a Nomination and if successful to fill up, in due course, the Entry Forms. The Conditions of a Retriever Trial are sometimes rather perplexing to the novice, and should be studied carefully. Mistakes cause a great deal of unnecessary correspondence and waste of time. *Nota bene*, spare the unpaid Secretary as much as possible !

That a dog requires any particular form of training to be successful at Trials, I do not for one moment believe. Naturally, he must be a good Retriever, fulfilling as far as possible the points as laid down in the Rules for the Trial Meetings (paragraph 3), already printed in this Chapter. But that he must be taught any special tricks—other than a really good Retriever should know—is not the case.

Where a dozen, more or less, picked Retrievers are brought together, good style in retrieving and quickness is sure to count in favour of a dog possessing these qualities. Again, marking fallen game, going well out from his handler (when ordered to do so) and working cleverly to the wave of an arm or whistle signal, are all signs of sagacity.

These points cannot be ignored in judging, but at the same time handlers and judges must both bear in mind that Trials are organised to find out the *best* Retrievers at the Meeting, not the best *broken* or handled animal. One does not require the man to find the game and then direct his dog to its whereabouts.

Although prizes are generally offered for good handling it is the dogs that should count first; and Judges give the preference to "nose" above all other qualifications.

Nowadays, it is very unlikely that a slow Retriever will win a Stake unless he is very superior at game finding to the other competing animals, and therefore in choosing a dog to run at Trials a certain amount of importance must be attached to quickness. But pace can be overdone and in the opinion of several good authorities this has already taken place. No Retriever should go faster than his nose permits him to do. A galloping, showy dog that passes dead game should be heavily penalised, no matter how brilliant is his style and dash.

Several instances occur to my mind of dogs and handlers, both complete novices as far as Retriever Trials are concerned, appearing at a Meeting and returning home winners.

This fully bears out my statement that a Retriever does not require any special form of training to enable him to get into the Prize List.

Naturally, good handling very materially helps him, but if a dog is a good Retriever, really well broken, and with an aptitude to catch runners, he has as much chance as any old Field Trial stager.

Of course, experience in handling must not be ignored, and an experienced Field Trial handler will often make a very good show with an indifferent Retriever which, in the hands of a novice, would fail miserably. I say, guardedly, indifferent Retriever, because no handler, however good he is, will win prizes with a bad Retriever, at least not under the class of Judges who have hitherto acted at Meetings.

In selecting a possible candidate for Retriever Trial honours I should feel inclined to acquire one whose forbears have acquitted themselves well at Trials, although this is a matter that can be left open. All the same, there have been some notable examples of certain winning dogs begetting much winning stock and this should not be ignored.

My advice to handlers will be brief and I am afraid not very instructive. When new to the procedure of a Trial Meeting, naturally you will have something to learn, both in the method of conducting it and how the work is judged.

You cannot do better at first than keep a watchful eye on other handlers (especially on those whom you may have learnt are experts), noting well their methods of working their dogs.

The chances are that you will remark nothing different to what you are accustomed to do yourself. So much the better. I have already mentioned that at Trials more time and latitude is given to the dogs than in an ordinary day's shooting; or, in other words, that a Retriever is given every opportunity to find his game before a Judge orders him to be recalled.

A good Judge is capable of seeing if the dog is out of hand, and therefore you need not be afraid of letting him get well out from you, if necessary.

Disturbing fresh ground at Trials is not as heinous an offence as it is when merely shooting for the bag.

A gamekeeper of my acquaintance on being asked what he thought of the work done at some recent Trials, which he had attended as a spectator for the first time, replied that " he didn't think much of it," and on being pressed for further particulars stated that the dogs were evidently trained to do what he had been taught from his earliest times to avoid, namely, to range wide and break fresh ground. This criticism, although severe, can be justified, as my friend evidently forgot that the object of the work was to produce the best Retriever, and that calling a dog off when working up to a strong runner would not be the way to arrive at any satisfactory decision. Besides a well broken Retriever should be capable of being worked either close in to his handler, or the reverse, according to circumstances.

Should your Retriever commit some enormity, such as chasing or failing ignominiously to find an easy dead bird, your chances of a win will naturally be handicapped, but a mistake of this kind has before now (especially at Local Trials) been partially eclipsed by some subsequent brilliant work. Therefore take heart and persevere to the end.

Remember, also, that a proportion of dogs must be weeded out during the day, and should your faithful " Rover " be among the number who " will not be required again by the Judges," solace yourself with the thought that good as " Rover " is, there may yet be better ones.

Possibly the final awards may not meet with your approval, but remember that it is impossible for you to have judged *all* the work that has been done and that six eyes are better than two.

Trials for Retrievers have most certainly been the cause of resuscitating a decaying breed and putting new vigour into its work. They give opportunity for friendly competition and also are an encouragement to keepers to break Retrievers. While finally, competitors, whether they win or lose will, I am positive, have their dogs' work judged without partiality, favour, or affection.

———————

CHAPTER V.

Kennel Management.

SO many far more able pens than mine have written on kennel management that I have not the inclination, nor do I think it necessary, to write more than a few words on this very important subject. In order to get the best results possible from dogs of any breed, they should be healthy and well cared for, and although I do not advocate the pampering of dogs in any way, I think that a certain amount of care and good management, especially in kennels of working dogs, are necessary.

In the first place, as regards Retrievers, do not keep more dogs than you can use or house properly. If you do not adhere to this maxim, the majority of them will probably suffer from want of work, exercise, and individual attention. Retrievers, if they are to perform well in the field, require more or less regular work, according to their individual dispositions. The endeavour to make four dogs do work which two could easily manage, generally results in suffering to all four. In some kennels, of course, in addition to the Retrievers which are actually

K

used in the field, there are often others which for
various reasons are not expected to come out regularly, such as bitches used for breeding purposes (we
hope after having been shot over for a season or
two) and youngsters of various ages. A kennel
of these dimensions on a shooting estate would
probably be divided up among the keepers, and
where this is the case a brace of Retrievers is sufficient for one man to use at work. If he has other
animals also to look after, care must be taken that
the accommodation is sufficient and good.

Working Retrievers (as distinct from brood bitches
and puppies) should generally be kept in their kennels.
By this I mean, not that they should never be taken
out, but that they should not be allowed to roam about
by themselves or become family pets. If permitted
their freedom, they nearly always get lazy, and sometimes fat, and often learn a lot of bad tricks.
Naturally, I have known several exceptions to this,
but taken broadly the above holds good.

And now a word about keepers' kennels. I have
seen Retrievers domiciled in various places, from the
humble tubs to the magnificent structures built
expressly for them, and my experience teaches me
that it is not always the occupants of these palatial
surroundings who look the best in health. No kennel,
of course, must be damp or draughty, and kennels
should periodically be thoroughly washed and freed

from vermin. A scrubbing-brush, some strong soap and hot water, with a little McDougall's sheep-dip in it, are quite sufficient to keep clean any ordinary wooden kennel or kennel bench, which should be washed at least three or four times a year, days being selected when they will dry quickly, before their occupants are returned to them. The walls of brick kennels should be whitewashed annually at least, and the floors well swilled down and scrubbed with hot water and sheep-dip at the same time that the bench is washed.

I am not a believer in the constant washing of kennels, whether they be of wood, brick, or any other material. If so treated in all weathers, they are bound before long to become damp. Dogs that are properly exercised, especially in the mornings and evenings, learn very cleanly habits, and a well-managed kennel requires, therefore, but little tidying up each day.

A kennel and its adjoining yard or ground should have all droppings removed twice daily, and a little sawdust, sprinkled on the wet places, will help greatly to keep it clean.

Wooden kennels in the open, to which dogs are chained up, should be periodically removed to fresh ground. Apart from sanitary reasons, the ground underneath the kennel gets very damp if the kennel stands a long time in one place. Straw or coarse

shavings make the best bedding ; in warm weather
these can be dispensed with, and the kennels and
benches can then more easily be kept free from
insects.

It is quite useless to put a dirty dog into a clean
kennel; therefore dogs also should be periodically
washed, not only for their own comfort and health's
sake, but also for the comfort of anyone who has to
do with them. It is not sufficient merely to let a
Retriever have occasional swims in a river or pond.
A working Retriever should be washed about every
three or four months, and to be of any use the washing
must be done thoroughly. A piece of Spratt's dog
soap should be used for choice, or, failing that,
common yellow soap, provided a small quantity of
McDougall's sheep-dip is used in the hot water. This
sheep-dip must, however, be used with caution, as its
properties are very strong; it contains, I believe,
among other things carbolic acid. A small lump
about the size of a pigeon's egg, dissolved in two
ordinary buckets of hot water, is the quantity I
recommend. If used in larger proportions it may
cause the animal much suffering. I have an impression, also, that a Retriever's nose suffers for a day or
two after a bath in sheep-dip—the smell of it rather
hangs about him for several hours afterwards. Nevertheless it is an excellent and cheap disinfectant for
the skin. Examine the dog carefully, especially in

summer time, to see that no sheep ticks are fixed into his skin, and always dry the *inside* of the ears carefully after a bath. Immediately after he has been washed, the dog should be exercised ; he should not be put back all wet into his kennel. No dog is really comfortable and healthy unless he is, from time to time, freed from the insects from which he is unable to free himself.

Unless absolutely necessary, do not wash puppies, but dust their coats well with Keating's insect powder, rubbing it in thoroughly down to the skin. These tasks are not very hard to carry out, and all keepers should make their performance a rule. The healthy appearance of a Retriever rests very much on the state of his coat, and anyone in charge of dogs should take enough pride in them to make them look their best—just as a good stud groom tries to turn out his master's horses well groomed and trimmed up. In addition to an occasional washing, Retrievers require a small amount of attention with a comb, in order to remove all dead hair, which otherwise becomes brown and matted. A man who will take the trouble to run the comb over his dogs for five minutes twice a week, will do a great deal towards giving them that shining and healthy appearance which looks so well. If he really aims at a higher standard of perfection, he can use a dandy brush or hound glove in addition; the comb I

consider a necessity, which should be kept in every
well-organised kennel, just as collars and chains are
kept.   One of Spratt's steel combs can be bought
for one shilling and sixpence, so cost cannot be
pleaded as an excuse for its absence. The subject of
chains reminds me that, when out shooting, all young
Retrievers should be chained up during the luncheon
hour.   Chains are preferable to a cord or slip, as
young dogs very soon acquire the habit of gnawing
through cord, and when once learnt the practice is
never forgotten.

A young Retriever, roaming loose around a farm-
house or cottage, is very likely to get into some mischief, either by foraging for himself in unsuitable
places or by going into fowl-houses and such-like
spots where vermin abounds.   No Retriever—
whether old or young—should be permitted to
move about while luncheon is in progress. Dogs,
whether begging for morsels in the open or
entering the house if luncheon is indoors, are
generally voted a nuisance. Make your Retriever
sit down quietly, and if he behaves himself reward
him afterwards.

The subject of food for dogs is a very important
one, but it is far too big to discuss here. I must
therefore unwillingly pass it over, merely remarking
that whatever food is selected it should be of
good quality, well prepared, and given in suitable

quantities. In addition to this, there should be frequent variety.

If two dogs are kennelled together, it generally happens that one of them gets the larger share of the food—that is, if both are loose in the kennel. In order to remedy this, when food is given, the animal that has the more greedy appetite should be chained up, out of reach of the other dog's pan. I do not believe in removing the remainder of the food as soon as the dog finishes feeding; many dogs which eat slowly will clean out their pan before morning comes. I always keep gross feeders chained all night—a ring being fixed in the wall close to the bench. The animal that eats the larger quantity is generally the older dog, so the chain probably does not cause any material damage. As a general rule, I am averse to chaining up dogs in their kennel, as I think they are more comfortable when loose, and chains undoubtedly make young dogs' elbows and feet turn out.

For the same reason that I have avoided the subject of feeding, I must skip over their medical treatment—merely laying stress on one or two of the most important points. Retrievers, if managed on careful and intelligent lines, do not require, as a rule, much doctoring. There are, however, exceptions to every rule, and the chief exceptions in this case are the treatment for distemper and worms. Practically all dogs suffer from these two troubles at some periods of their lives; they sometimes escape the former, but never, I think, the latter.

A good number of cases of distemper have come under my notice, and I cannot help thinking that the disease is very similar to what we human beings call influenza. Most of us know the distemper symptoms in dogs: they are generally identical with those of influenza, although both maladies take all sorts of forms. But the chief characteristics are always present; that is, the dog in distemper is off his feed, runs at the nose, and if we take his temperature with a clinical thermometer *per rectum*, we shall find that it is more or less high. As in most cases of sickness, good nursing is the most important part of the cure. The dog must be constantly attended to, kept clean, warm, and in a kennel with an even temperature (if possible) of about fifty degrees day and night. Chills, which often prove fatal, can be avoided by sewing his body up in a piece of house flannel. His strength must be kept up by good, light feeding, such as strong soup mixed with boiled rice or bread, warm milk, etc., and these must be put down his throat if he won't feed himself. In extreme cases, where a dog gets so weak that he cannot stand, a couple of raw eggs beaten up with a teaspoonful of brandy should be given every three or four hours. As regards the medicines, there are dozens of "*cures*" offered on the market, some of which are described as infallible; but, with all due deference to the vendors, I cannot agree that they are entitled to this description. So far, within my experience, no medicine has been discovered for the *cure* of this disease, and the same applies to the various *serums* advertised. Until the bacillus of distemper has been located, I doubt if any cure will be found beyond that of good nursing. In distemper cases my primary objective is to reduce the feverish temperature of the dog by means of *febrifuges*, such as salicylate of soda, quinine, or antipyrin, and when once you have got the temperature to remain normal for more than twenty-four hours, you can reckon that the poison of the disease is losing its power, and that the patient is on the mend. Great care, however, must be taken not to allow him to run any risks of chills or over-exertion. A relapse is a very dangerous thing.

The medicines and treatment that I give are as follows :—

Give the dog about half a table-spoonful of castor-oil before the treatment is commenced, and after the effects of it have worked off the following should be tried :—

Salicine . } of each . 72 grains.
Salicylate of soda }

Water to . . . . 6 ounces.

Dose.—From one teaspoonful to a tablespoonful (according to the age and size of the dog) every four hours, day and night.

If the above does not lower the temperature after three or four days' treatment it should be discontinued, and one of the following remedies can be substituted :—

Give from one to five grains (according to the age and size of the dog) of *sulphate of quinine* every six hours, or from two to eight grains of *antipyrin*.

The first of these two medicines can be administered best in gelatine capsules, which can be filled by the chemist to the required doses, whilst the second can be bought in the form of tabloids.

Coughing can be relieved by giving from five to twenty drops of paregoric, mixed with the same quantity of syrup of squills.

After the temperature has become permanently normal, the dog will require light, strengthening food, and possibly a tonic in the shape of Parrish's food or a medicine with iron in it. The normal temperature of a dog, taken in the bowel, is 101°, but in distemper it rises sometimes to 106°.

When dealing with a large subject like the cure of distemper, these instructions are, of course, somewhat meagre, but I have roughly given the outline of my own method of treatment, in case it should be of any service (especially to keepers).

For some of my knowledge I am indebted to *Dogs : Their Management*, by the late E. Mayhew, M.R.C.V.S., partly rewritten by A. J. Sewell, M.R.C.V.S. This is an excellent work on dog diseases, and should be in the possession of all who take an interest in canine matters.

The other exception that I mentioned was worms in the intestines of dogs. It may be taken for granted that nine puppies out of ten are infested with round worms almost from the time they are weaned, and that all mature dogs suffer from worms (tapeworms generally) unless steps are taken to remove them. To puppies, unless a cure is effected, the disease often proves fatal, or at any rate the puppy's health suffers severely. These abominable parasites bring on fits, constipation, and many other ailments, which are often described by the ignorant as due to distemper. Soon after puppies are weaned, which is generally when they are six or seven weeks old, they should be dosed periodically, which dosing generally results in a large number of worms being expelled. The usual method is to feed the puppies somewhat lightly and rather earlier than usual, and to give the doses the following morning on an empty stomach. *Santonine* and *castor-oil* are very good remedies, and should be given in the following doses for Retriever puppies :—

To puppies from six to seven weeks old, three-quarters of a grain mixed in a teaspoonful of castor-oil. When the puppies are ten or twelve weeks old, the quantity of santonine may be doubled.

Half an hour after the medicine has been given, the puppies should have a little *warm* soup or milk, and then be allowed to run about.

The santonine can be procured from any good chemist, and, to save trouble, should be made up in separate papers—each paper containing one dose. These papers which contain the powder should be stored in a more or less air-tight box. Puppies should be treated in this way twice a week, until all signs of worms have disappeared. And the treatment should be repeated about once a month, until the puppies are four months old.

There are, of course, several patent worm medicines offered for sale, and the efficacy of many of them is equal to that of santonine.

The greatest attention in this respect should be given to all puppies which are sent out at walk. Scores of valuable foxhound puppies, without doubt, annually fail to return from quarters owing entirely to absence of this attention. Every puppy that is put out at walk should be treated periodically from home, or full directions and medicine should be sent out with him. Mature dogs should also from time to time be treated for tapeworm, whether they show any signs of having them or not. As a rule, the presence of tapeworm in a dog is perceptible to an observant person, although some dogs appear perfectly well and healthy, in spite of the fact that they are troubled with these parasites. My own plan is, roughly, to treat all mature dogs for tapeworm about twice a year, and even then I find that it is almost impossible to keep a kennel entirely free from the pest. I don't think, however, that these tapeworms cause the dog much inconvenience until they reach a certain size; nevertheless they should be removed whenever there is the slightest suspicion of their presence. The only means of doing this is to dose the dog about every six months. He must be kept *absolutely* without food of any sort for twenty-four hours before the medicine is administered. In fact, he should not be taken out to exercise on the previous day, lest he should pick up food.

Fortunately, tapeworms are easy to get rid of temporarily, and either of the two following prescriptions will work its purpose.

Give freshly ground *areca nut* in the following quantities :—

Dogs, four months old			.	.	20 grains.
,,	six	,,	,,	.	.	30 ,,
,,	nine	,,	,,	.	.	40 ,,
,,	one year		,,	.	.	60 ,,

These doses should be given after the dog has fasted from twelve to twenty-four hours previously (according to the age of the animal) mixed either in a little butter or in milk. Half a grain of santonine can often be added with advantage to the above doses.

About an hour afterwards, give the dog from a teaspoonful to two and a half teaspoonfuls (according to age and size) of castor-oil.

Some warm soup or milk should be given half an hour after the latter medicine has been administered, and the dog should then be taken out for exercise. In order to effect a *certain* cure, this treatment should be repeated again in a week's time.

Kamala is another remedy, and the doses are the same as those recommended for areca nut. Remember that areca nut must be freshly grated, which is a rather tedious operation. An ordinary farrier's rasp should be kept for this purpose, the nut, when it becomes too small to be held between the fingers, being crushed up fine with a hammer.

It may be useful to know that, roughly speaking, an ordinary-sized teaspoon will contain twenty grains of grated areca nut—the powder being on a level with the edges of the spoon. In measuring out liquids, it can be taken as a general rule, that one tablespoonful of liquid weighs half an ounce.

These rough measurements will always suffice for harmless drugs, but, when any prescription in the shape of a poison is being made up, the measurements cannot be too accurate.

If a dog is easy to dose, one man can administer the medicine without any assistance; but some dogs, especially old ones, are at times rather difficult to manage, and it may require two people—one man to hold the dog's head, while the other gives the medicine. Whether the dog submits quietly or not, do not be rough with him in any way, but handle him gently. The dog's muzzle should be slightly raised, and one of the underlips should be gently drawn out. The medicine can then be poured, a little at a time, into the " pocket " formed by the underlip. It will run through the dog's teeth, and, if the muzzle is kept held up, will find its way down his throat. If he refuses to swallow, place one hand over his nostrils, and he will take the medicine when in the act of breathing through his mouth. After being dosed, a dog's muzzle should be firmly tied up with tape, and he should be chained up in such a position that he cannot put his head close to the ground and vomit up the medicine. He need only be kept like this for about a quarter of an hour, after which he may be released.

This all reads as though it were a very serious undertaking, but, if performed carefully and quietly, it is far simpler to do than to describe.

These methods, of course, are not necessary for puppies, and by far the easiest way in which to give medicine to any dog (if in small quantities) is by means of gelatine capsules, which can be gently pushed down into the throat.

Canker or inflammation of the ear is often a source of trouble, especially in sporting kennels. Any signs of it should at once be attended to, as, if the disease gets a firm hold, it is very likely to become chronic. Dog's ears should from time to time be examined to see whether they are clean and cool inside. If, on lifting the flap of the ear, you notice any signs of heat and redness, it is quite time you treated the dog medically. Apart from any heat, you should not allow the inside of your dog's ears to remain dirty; unless attended to occasionally, they become very blocked up and unsightly, with a brown caked discharge which often brings on inflammation. A dog which has his ears occasionally cleaned and dressed inside rarely, if ever, suffers from canker, even in extreme old age.

The operation of cleaning a dog's ears, after they have been neglected some time, is rather lengthy, but if they are periodically cleaned much time and trouble will be saved. Put a tablespoonful of methylated spirits into a cup of warm water, and provide yourself with a short piece of wood, about the same length and thickness as an ordinary penholder. Cut a cleft into the blunt end and firmly insert into this cleft a piece of absorbent cotton wool, to act as a cleaning wad. Dip this cotton wool constantly in the warm water and thoroughly clean the inside of the dog's ear, gently pushing the wad of cotton wool well down into the ear. Change the cotton wool whenever it becomes too dirty. Then dry the inside of the ears thoroughly, by inserting a dry piece of cotton wool in the same manner.

Next fill the inside of the ears with boracic acid or iodoform powder, either pushing the powder well down into the ear with the stick and dry wad, or blowing it into the ear by means of a piece of small indiarubber tubing. All dogs' ears should occasionally be dressed in this manner. This treatment, when adopted in time, will cure mild cases of canker, but if the case is neglected it will become a much more serious matter. The treatment is very simple, and no one can complain of it on the score of expense, as enough boracic acid powder, absorbent wool, etc., can be bought for a shilling to treat scores of dogs.

In more serious cases of canker, clean the dogs' ears thoroughly in the manner described, and when dry turn the ear upwards, and drop in a little canker lotion, manipulating the base of them

L

gently with the hand, so as to work the lotion well inside.

This canker lotion can be bought of Mr. A. S. Campkin, Chemist, 11, Rose Crescent, Cambridge, and is sold in various-sized bottles, from one shilling upwards.

In addition to the treatment I have described, a mild purgative should be given to a dog which shows signs of inflammation inside his ears.

For a full-grown Retriever a tablespoonful of castor-oil, or of Epsom salts, is an ordinary dose ; the salts should be well mixed with two or three tablespoonfuls of water.

If the dog continually shakes his head, especially when first let loose from his kennel, inflammation inside the ear is probable. In severe cases, I believe, the discharge and inflammation are accompanied by a very offensive smell.

A mild purgative should always be given to bitches when in use, and not wanted for breeding purposes. Their ordinary exercise is always curtailed, and they therefore occasionally require some laxative dose, such as Epsom salts, and at the same time should be fed lightly. If it is necessary to work a bitch who is either coming into use or just going off, it is a good plan to smear a small quantity of carbolic oil or tar ointment on her quarters. This slight dressing will generally prevent undue attention on the part of other dogs. Bitches, however, when in this state, should not be worked if it can possibly be avoided. They usually work in a very slack manner, and are also a source of great annoyance if other dogs are in the field.

Retrievers especially suffer from " spectacles " or dryness of skin round the eyelids. The hair nearly always comes off, and the dog looks unsightly. This is sometimes, though not always, a sign of tapeworm. The eyelids should never be neglected, but should be sponged occassionally with water, in which a little boracic acid powder has been dissolved. A teaspoonful of boracic acid powder mixed with twelve tablespoonfuls of water is a good proportion, and should be kept ready for use in a bottle. In addition to this, a pot of ointment should be in every kennel and the eyelids of all dogs suffering from " spectacles " should be dressed with either of the following dressings, which are excellent, and will remain good for an indefinite time.

GOULARD'S OINTMENT

Yellow resin	$\frac{1}{4}$ oz.
Prepared lard	1 oz.
Goulard's Extract . . .	1 oz.

Melt the resin and lard with a gentle heat, and stir in the extract.

Boracic Acid Ointment

Boracic acid (in fine powder)   .   .   1 oz.
Paraffin ointment   .   .   .   7 oz.

Mix well together.

The above are also good dressings to rub on to any bare places where the skin requires softening.

Mange and eczema in dogs are two totally different diseases, but in their earlier stages, at least, it requires an expert to distinguish between them.

Not being versed in veterinary lore, I will therefore merely explain my treatment of Retrievers, whose skins require attention in a minor degree. Whenever a dog is seen to have a breaking out on his skin—the elbows and inside of the thighs are often the first places attacked—steps should at once be taken to check further progress. Give the animal a mild purgative of castor-oil or Epsom salts, and then dress the affected parts with one of the following :—

Glycerole of subacetate of lead   .   1 drachm.
Vaseline   .   .   .   1 oz.

To be well mixed and gently rubbed on the parts affected, twice a day.

Or, if there is much discharge, use the following :—

Powdered boracic acid
Pure oxide of zinc   .   } in equal parts.
Flowers of sulphur   .

Mix these together, and powder the raw places constantly.

Continue this treatment until all signs of the discharge have disappeared, and then dress the affected places daily with Goulard's or boracic acid ointment.

When the dog's skin is badly affected he must be dressed all over, and in such cases my general treatment is this :—

Mix eight tablespoonfuls of flowers of sulphur with one pint of olive oil. This mixture should be put in a large bottle and thoroughly well shaken before being applied. It must be well rubbed into the dog's skin, not only on the affected parts, but all over the body, every other day for a week. Then thoroughly wash the dog with soap and warm water. The following day repeat the process and continue for another week, at the end of which time wash the dog again. It is a good plan also to give the animal a tablespoonful of Epsom salts twice during the above treatment.

M

Another good dressing for the skin is the following :—

Flowers of sulphur	4 oz.
Oil of tar	1 oz.
Oil of turpentine	$\frac{1}{4}$ oz.
Olive oil	1 pint.

Mix well together and shake before using.

The treatment is the same, except that I usually leave this dressing on for about ten days, and then wash the dog thoroughly, as a second dressing is generally not required.

The disease of yellows, I am thankful to say, has so far avoided my kennel ; therefore I cannot write of it from experience. It is a dangerous disease, similar to jaundice in the human being, and is due generally to a chill on the liver. I take the liberty of copying the following prescription from Mr. W. Arkwright's book, *The Pointer and his Predecessors :*—

" Put one good handful of barberry bark into a quart of strong ale, boiling. Administer three table-spoonfuls, three times a day, adding a teaspoonful of nitre to each dose."

The general nursing should be the same as in cases of distemper.

A Retriever with a good constitution, if treated in a humane and rational manner, is usually one of the healthiest animals that a man could wish to possess. Owners of dogs, therefore, would do well to inquire into matters if they notice that their animals have a neglected appearance, which invariably means that they are not in a healthy state.

Appended is a list of articles which should be kept in every kennel—large or small. The quantities being in proportion to the number of dogs kept.

Castor-oil.	Epsom salts.
Goulard's ointment.	Boracic acid ointment.
Areca nuts.	Boracic acid powder.
Dog soap.	McDougall's sheep-dip.

Leather muzzle.	Tape.	Tablespoon.
House flannel.	Clinical thermometer.	
Farriers' rasp.	Medical minim glass.	

Any other medicines or dressings can be procured as required from the local chemist, but those I have named should always be at hand.

I feel bound to quit my subject now—possibly to the relief of some readers, should they have waded on thus far. A shooting man or keeper who possesses a first-class working Retriever is much to be envied, and any little extra trouble entailed in producing and keeping such a dog is not trouble wasted. In addition to being indispensable to a shooting man, they are good friends and honest servants.

> "*I like to think of the work you've done,*
> *And the shoots we've had together;*
> *The good and bad, the big and small,*
> *The scent, the fur, the feather.*
> *Sad shall I be when Death steps in—*
> *That monster grim and cold;*
> *For nothing else shall part us, Jack—*
> *No, not your weight in gold!*"

If the foregoing notes prove of any assistance to owners or handlers, I shall be quite repaid for the time and ink that I. have devoted to a topic which has already been dealt with by others, but into which I have tried to introduce new matter.

INDEX.

Printed in the United Kingdom
by Lightning Source UK Ltd.
113034UKS00001B/47